MENTAL HEALTH LAW
IN A NUTSHELL®

JOHN E.B. MYERS
Professor of Law
University of the Pacific
McGeorge School of Law

WEST
ACADEMIC
PUBLISHING

© 2016 LEG, Inc. d/b/a West Academic
      444 Cedar Street, Suite 700
      St. Paul, MN 55101
      1-877-888-1330

West, West Academic Publishing, and West Academic are trademarks of West Publishing Corporation, used under license.

Printed in the United States of America

ISBN: 978-1-63459-889-7

OUTLINE

TABLE OF CASES

References are to Pages

MENTAL
HEALTH LAW
IN A NUTSHELL®

CHAPTER 1
INTRODUCTION

What is mental health law? The answer is: Many things to many people. This Nutshell covers a broad range of subjects at the interface of law, psychology, clinical social work, psychiatry, and medicine. Subjects include the insanity defense, the Americans with Disabilities Act, involuntary psychiatric hospitalization, Social Security disability, and much more.

Most Nutshell readers are law students or lawyers who have relatively little training in psychology, apart from a course or two in college. For that reason, Chapter 1 begins with an introduction to the mental health professions and mental health diagnosis and practice.

A.   MENTAL HEALTH PROFESSIONALS

Mental health services are provided by clinical social workers, psychologists, psychiatrists, nurses, and various categories of counselors. Each profession is regulated by statute, regulation, and government agencies, and requires a license. Licensure requires university training, usually at the masters or doctoral level, many hours of supervised clinical experience, and passage of a test that covers ethics, law, and mental health theory and practice. (*See Texas State Board of Examiners of Marriage and Family Therapists v. Texas Medical Association*, 458 S.W.3d 552 (Tex. Ct. App. 2014)).

Social workers work in many settings, including child protection, hospitals, jails, schools, welfare agencies, and in mental health. Licensed clinical social workers (LCSW) earn a master's degree in social work (MSW) or a doctorate (Ph.D. or D.S.W.), and provide psychotherapy, counseling, and other services for clients in hospitals, mental health clinics, and in private office practice.

Psychologists work in many settings. Clinical psychologists provide psychotherapy. Psychologists administer and interpret intelligence tests, personality assessments, and other standardized psychological measures. Most formal psychological testing is performed by psychologists. Educational psychologists provide psychological testing, diagnosis, assessment, and counseling for students.

A psychiatrist is a medical doctor who completes a residency in psychiatry after medical school. Because psychiatrists are physicians, they have authority to prescribe medications. Although there is movement to allow doctoral level psychologists to administer certain medications, most medications in the mental health context are prescribed by psychiatrists and other physicians.

Psychiatric nurses are registered nurses (RN) who take special training in mental health. Some psychiatric nurses are licensed to provide psychotherapy.

Marriage and family therapists (MFT) are clinicians who earn a masters or doctoral degree in counseling, psychology, or a closely related field. MFTs conduct therapy with individuals, but often focus their work on groups, couples, and families.

States have additional categories of mental health professionals, including, for example, Licensed Professional Counselor.

Licensed mental health professionals, like attorneys, are required to participate in continuing education programs.

States have procedures to suspend and revoke licenses for unprofessional and criminal conduct. An accused professional has a right to dispute accusations at a hearing before an administrative law judge or in court.

In addition to being licensed by the state, many mental health professionals belong to professional organizations, including the National Association of Social Workers (NASW), American Psychological Association (APA), American Psychiatric Association, American Nurses Association (ANA), and others. Professional organizations impose discipline or exclude members who commit ethical or legal violations.

Some mental health professionals specialize in forensic practice, defined by the American Psychological Association as "applying the scientific, technical, or specialized knowledge of psychology to the law to assist in addressing legal, contractual, and administrative matters." (American Psychological Association, *Specialty Guidelines for Forensic Psychology* (2013)). The American Academy of Psychiatry and Law (AAPL) defines forensic practice as "a subspecialty of psychiatry in which scientific and clinical expertise is applied in legal contexts involving civil, criminal, correctional, regulatory, or legislative matters, and in specialized clinical consultations in areas such as risk assessment or employment." (AAPL, *Ethics Guidelines for the Practice of Forensic Psychiatry*). Examples of forensic mental health practice include assessments regarding competence to stand trial, the insanity defense, child custody evaluations, and preparing various reports for courts.

Of the many publications on forensic psychology, two leading treatises are Brian L. Cutler & Patricia A. Zapf (Eds.), *American Psychological Association Handbook of Forensic Psychology* (2015), and Gary B. Melton, John Petrila, Norman G. Poythress & Christopher Slobogin, *Psychological Evaluations for the Courts: A Handbook for Mental Health Professionals and Lawyers* (2d ed. 1997).

Not all court involvement by mental health professionals is forensic practice. Thus, a clinician who sees clients in psychotherapy, and who does not regularly appear in court, is not practicing forensic psychology when the therapist testifies about a particular client.

B. DIFFERENCES BETWEEN MENTAL HEALTH AND LEGAL PROFESSIONALS

Mental health and legal professionals work to improve the human condition. Despite shared goals, however, mental health and legal professionals have different philosophies and methods. Not infrequently, mental health and legal professionals fail to see eye-to-eye. Indeed, psychologist Gary

Melton and his colleagues opine, "The philosophical assumptions that govern these disciplines seem, to a large extent, mutually exclusive." (Gary B. Melton, John Petrila, Norman G. Poythress & Christopher Slobogin, *Psychological Evaluations for the Courts: A Handbook for Mental Health Professionals and Lawyers* § 1.03(a), p. 9 (2d ed. 1997)).

Dora Klein describes one aspect of the complex relationship between law and psychology:

> Mental states are central to criminal law, so clinical psychology is, at least to some extent, an indispensable ally. But the ultimate goals of criminal law and clinical psychology are not the same. Clinical psychology aims to understand and to alter mental states, while criminal law usually is more concerned with determining the existence of particular mental states at particular points in time. Clinical psychology wants to know what caused the delusional belief and how to alleviate it, while criminal law wants to know if the delusional belief precluded knowledge of an act's wrongfulness or interfered with understanding the reason for a death sentence. Clinical psychology disclaims moral judgments, while criminal law is fundamentally a moral enterprise.

Dora W. Klein, The Mentally Disordered Criminal Defendant at the Supreme Court: A Decade in Review, 91 *Oregon Law Review* 207–245, at pp. 207–208 (2012).

Clinical mental health blends science, theory, and clinical knowledge toward the goals of preventing and alleviating psychologically-based distress and illness. The aim is the well-being of clients and the community. Mental health professionals subscribe to a broad range of theories of behavior, mental illness, and treatment, including psychoanalysis, originating with Sigmund Freud in the early 20th Century, humanistic treatment pioneered by Carl Rogers, cognitive behavioral therapy, systems therapy, and other theories and techniques.

In clinical practice, there is a movement toward evidence-based treatment. A treatment is evidence-based when it is supported by research. Cognitive behavior therapy (CBT), for example, is supported by a large body of empirical research that supports the efficacy of CBT. Thus, CBT is evidence-based.

Turning from clinical practice to law, law is premised on the rule of law set forth in constitutions, statutes, and appellate court decisions. Lawyers and judges interpret and enforce the law. Law and its practitioners do not ignore science, but law is not based on science or empirical research. When a lawyer says a case is evidence-based, the lawyer is talking about something quite different than a clinician using evidence-based therapeutic techniques.

In addition to philosophical differences, the methods of mental health professionals and lawyers differ. Mental health outcomes are achieved in the highly confidential setting of individual and group therapy. When appropriate, clients are prescribed medications to help with psychological symptoms. In law, outcomes are achieved through investigation, negotiation, compromise, mediation, arbitration, settlement, and, when necessary, litigation.

Litigation "is society's last line of defense in the indispensable effort to secure the peaceful settlement of social conflicts." (Henry Hart & John McNaughton, *Evidence and Inference in the Law*, p. 52 (1958)). For those trained in law, litigation is second nature. Indeed, for experienced litigators, court is home-away-from-home. Just the opposite is true for mental health professionals, many of whom find court intimidating. The hard edge of litigation, particularly cross-examination, is foreign to mental health professionals, whose training and philosophy point away from confrontation. Mental health professionals occasionally find themselves thinking, "Lawyers are a strange bunch. How do they expect to find the truth when they spend half the time hiding it from each other, and the other half obfuscating the facts with technical squabbles?" There is an old joke: "The kindly judge said to the witness, "You seem to be in some distress. Is anything the matter?" The witness replied, "Well, your honor, I swore to tell the truth, the whole truth, and nothing but the truth, but every time I try, some lawyer objects!"

Mental health and legal professionals inhabit different worlds. The goals of mental health professionals and lawyers often overlap, but the tools, knowledge, strategies, and mind set differ. For example, in a few years, you will be comfortable arguing before a judge. But how do you think you will feel if someone asks you to try your hand at psychotherapy? The experienced psychotherapist would be equally at a loss to write a persuasive brief for a court.

Although a gulf separates mental health from legal professionals, bridges must be built. Neither profession can achieve the maximum good for individuals and society alone. As a team, however, mental health professionals and lawyers accomplish a great deal.

C. IDIOT AND LUNATIC

An English statute from the middle ages defined individuals with mental disabilities as lunatics or idiots. (17 Edward 2, chapter 9–10 (1324)). A lunatic was a person whom today we would refer to as mentally ill. Lunatic comes from the Latin *luna*, the moon. The early thought was that mental illnesses come and go, like phases of the moon. Idiot was the term for those with intellectual disability, or, mental retardation, to use the older term.

D. DIAGNOSTIC AND STATISTICAL MANUAL OF MENTAL DISORDERS (DSM-5)

Today, mental illnesses and intellectual disabilities are described in the *Diagnostic and Statistical Manual of Mental Disorders* (5th ed. 2013), published by the American Psychiatric Association, (DSM–5). The DSM–5 is the "bible" of psychiatric diagnosis in the United States. The Illinois Supreme Court referred to the DSM as "an authoritative categorical classification of mental disorders." (*In re Detention of New*, 386 Ill. Dec. 643, 21 N.E.3d 406 (2014)). Similarly, the Mississippi Supreme Court wrote that DSM definitions may be used in court. (*Chase v. State*, 171 So. 3d 463 (Miss. 2015)).

The DSM–5 uses the term "mental disorder" rather than mental illness, and defines mental disorder as follows:

A mental disorder is a syndrome characterized by clinically significant disturbance in an individual's cognition, emotion regulation, or behavior that reflects a dysfunction in the psychological, biological, or developmental processes underlying mental functioning. Mental disorders are usually associated with significant distress or disability in social, occupational, or other important activities. An expectable or culturally approved response to a common stressor or loss, such as the death of a loved one, is not a mental disorder. Socially deviant behavior (*e.g.*, political, religious, or sexual) and conflicts that are primarily between the individual and society are not mental disorders unless the deviance or conflict results from a dysfunction in the individual, as described above. (p. 20).

Definitions of mental illness are not identical in law and psychology. For example, a person may be seriously mentally ill, as that term is used in the DSM–5, but not meet the definition of insanity in the insanity defense, or the legal standard for competence to stand trial, or to execute a will, or be eligible for Social Security disability benefits. The DSM–5 acknowledges "the imperfect fit between the questions of ultimate concern to the law and the information contained in a clinical diagnosis." (DSM–5, at p. 25). (*See* Carl E. Fisher, David L. Faigman & Paul S. Appelbaum, Toward a Jurisprudence of Psychiatric Evidence: Examining the Challenges of Reasoning from Group Data in Psychiatry to Individual Decisions in the Law, 69 *University of Miami Law Review* 685-753 (2015)).

To some degree, mental illness is a social construct: Society defines what conduct is normal and abnormal. Societal views about normality change. Thus, in the first edition of the DSM–1, published in 1952, homosexuality was listed as a mental disorder. Not so in the DSM–5. As homosexuality was accepted as normal, laws changed, including the right of gay and lesbian couples to marry. (*Obergefell v. Hodges,* 135 S. Ct. 2584 (2015)). Today, several states have laws prohibiting psychotherapy that is intended to alter sexual orientation, and such laws have withstood constitutional attack. (*Joe v. Governor of the State of New Jersey*, 783 F.3d 150 (3d Cir. 2015)).

E. SYNDROMES

Note that the DSM–5 defines a mental disorder as a syndrome. It is useful to understand the word syndrome. Expert testimony describing syndromes is common in court. A WestLaw search for the word syndrome in appellate cases revealed more than 10,000 hits!

The word syndrome was employed by Hippocrates, the father of medicine, in the fifth century B.C. The word appeared in medical treatises as early at 1541. Modernly, *Dorland's Medical Dictionary* defines syndrome as "a set of symptoms which occur together." (p. 1632, 28th ed. 1994). In medicine and mental health, syndromes are defined rather loosely. The *Encyclopedia of Medical Syndromes* states, "The definition of a syndrome is both vague and variable." (p. xiii, 1960).

The word syndrome should be compared to the word disease. *Dorland's Medical Dictionary* defines disease as "any deviation from or interruption of the normal structure or function of any part, organ, or system (or combination thereof) of the body that is manifested by a characteristic set of symptoms and signs and whose etiology, pathology, and prognosis may be known or unknown." (p. 528.)

The concepts of disease and syndrome overlap, but are not identical. With diseases, the cause—etiology—of a malady is often, although, not always, known. Thus, influenza is a disease that is produced by a specific virus, as is polio. With syndromes, by contrast, the cause/etiology of the patient's symptoms is often unknown or poorly understood. The *Encyclopedia of Medical Syndromes* describes the difference between diseases and syndromes as follows: "The terms syndrome and disease are often unwittingly used interchangeably although they are not synonymous. In general, a syndrome evokes more interest and is more challenging than a disease because its relationships are more obscure and its etiology is less apparent. If, subsequently, a specific etiologic factor does become manifest, the condition should then be reclassified as a disease." (p. xiii–ix).

F. SIGNS AND SYMPTOMS

A symptom is a subjective feeling reported by a patient. Thus, a patient in the Emergency Department following a traffic accident might say, "My leg really hurts, and I can't feel my toes." Or, "I'm nauseous." A client in a therapist's office might say, "I feel so sad lately."

A sign is an objective manifestation of illness or injury. For the Emergency Department patient mentioned above, signs of a broken leg include decreased mobility, swelling, and a displaced angle of the leg. For the psychotherapy client, signs of depression include flat affect and anhedonia (inability to feel pleasure).

In medical books, legal cases, and this book, the word symptom is often used to describe both symptoms and signs.

The law is preoccupied with causation: What caused an accident? What caused a victim's death? Etc. With the law's interest in causation, it is natural to ask, does the presence of a syndrome tend to prove what *caused* the person's signs and symptoms? The answer is: Sometimes. The presence of some syndromes provides evidence of their cause. Other syndromes, however, provide little or no evidence of causation.

Thus, some syndromes have what may be called "diagnostic value." The signs and symptoms making up the syndrome point to a particular cause or etiology. The clinician reasons: "In my patient, I observe signs and symptoms A, B, and C. These signs and symptoms comprise Syndrome Y. From the presence of Syndrome Y, I reason backward to the cause (etiology) of the symptoms. The ability to reason backward from signs and symptoms to cause is diagnostic value.

With some syndromes, the relationship between the signs and symptoms that make up the syndrome, and their etiology is clear. With many syndromes, however, the relationship between signs and symptoms and cause/etiology is unclear or unknown. When it is not possible to reason backward from signs and symptoms to etiology, the syndrome lacks diagnostic value.

Two syndromes that appear in court illustrate the presence and absence of diagnostic value: Battered Child Syndrome and Rape Trauma Syndrome. A child with Battered Child Syndrome is very likely to have suffered non-accidental injury. Battered Child Syndrome points convincingly to abuse. A doctor can reason backward from the signs and symptoms to the cause. Battered Child Syndrome has high diagnostic value. Judges routinely allow expert testimony on Battered Child Syndrome to prove child abuse. (*See* John E.B. Myers, *Myers on Evidence of Interpersonal Violence: Child Maltreatment, Intimate Partner*

Violence, Rape, Stalking, and Elder Abuse § 4.07 (6th ed. 2016)).

Compare the high diagnostic value of Battered Child Syndrome with Rape Trauma Syndrome, which has no diagnostic value. Rape Trauma Syndrome consists of symptoms and behaviors that are caused by a broad range of events including, but not limited to, rape. Rape Trauma Syndrome cannot be used to prove rape.

Most psychological syndromes lack diagnostic value. A DSM–5 diagnosis provides a great deal of information about a patient's signs and symptoms, but cannot be used to determine the origin/etiology of the signs and symptoms.

G. DIAGNOSING MENTAL ILLNESS

Diagnosing mental illness is the province of mental health and medical professionals. The word diagnosis has two meanings. First, diagnosis is the process of distinguishing one illness from another. Second, diagnosis describes the end result of the diagnostic process. Diagnosis is the label attached to a disease, syndrome, or condition.

The diagnostic process typically begins by taking a "history" from the patient. The diagnostician asks questions about the patient's past illnesses, injuries, hospitalizations, etc. The history provides background information to assist the professional in reaching a diagnosis. Of course, the history provided by patients is not always accurate, particularly if the patient is seriously ill, or has a motive to distort. A motive to distort may exist when the patient is involved in litigation. David Price observes, "Face-to-face interviews in and of themselves are not necessarily adequate for a valid mental diagnosis. Many diagnoses of psychiatric and psychological disorders in mental and emotional injury claims are accomplished solely via interview of the litigant and based upon the litigant's own self-reported symptoms, which can often result in error." (David R. Price, Clinical Evaluation and Case Formulation of Mental and Emotional Injury Claims. In James J. McDonald, Jr. & Francine B. Kulick, *Mental and Emotional Injuries in Employment Litigation,* p. 72 (2001)).

In mental health practice, an important part of the diagnostic process is the mental status examination. The professional asks questions to learn of the patient's current mental state and functioning. A helpful description of the mental status examination is found on the Social Security Administration's website that lists criteria to evaluate disabilities based on mental disorder. The website states:

> The mental status examination is performed in the course of a clinical interview and is often partly assessed while the history is being obtained. A comprehensive mental status examination generally includes a narrative description of your appearance, behavior, and speech; thought process (*e.g.*, loosening of associations); thought content (*e.g.*, delusions); perceptual abnormalities (*e.g.*, hallucinations); mood and affect (*e.g.*, depression, mania);

sensorium and cognition (*e.g.*, orientation, recall, memory, concentration, fund of information, and intelligence); and judgment and insight.

Differential diagnosis is the process of differentiating one disease, syndrome, or disorder from others. Ruling out alternative diagnoses allows the professional to zero in on the correct diagnosis. (*See State v. Consaul*, 332 P.3d 850 (N.M. 2014)). Diagnosis is fallible, a truism for physical disorders as well as mental disorders.

A patient's prognosis is a professional's estimate of the future course of the patient's disorder or disease. A prognosis is "guarded" when doubt surrounds the future.

H.   DSM-5 DISORDERS

The DSM–5 contains twenty-one categories of mental disorder, each with subcategories. The categories are briefly described below.

I.   NEURODEVELOPMENTAL DISORDERS

This category includes Intellectual Developmental Disorder (IDD), previously called mental retardation. The degree of intellectual impairment will be mild, moderate, severe, or profound. "The various levels of severity are defined on the basis of adaptive functioning and not IQ scores, because it is adaptive functioning that determines the level of supports required." (DSM–5, at p. 33).

Communication Disorders include difficulties with language, speech (*e.g.*, stuttering), and communication.

The hallmark of Autism Spectrum Disorder is "deficits in social communication and social interaction across multiple contexts." (DSM–5, at p. 50).

Attention-Deficit/Hyperactivity   Disorder manifests itself in "a persistent pattern of inattention and/or hyperactivity-impulsivity that interferes with functioning or development." (DSM–5, at p. 59).

Specific Learning Disorder is often called "learning disability," and brings to mind dyslexia, defined as "a pattern of learning difficulties characterized by problems with accurate or fluent word recognition, poor decoding, and poor spelling abilities." (DSM–5, at p. 67).

J. SCHIZOPHRENIA SPECTRUM DISORDER AND OTHER PSYCHOTIC DISORDERS

In popular parlance, the word "psychosis" is used to describe someone who is mentally ill and out of touch with reality. In fact, individuals suffering psychosis are seldom completely out of touch with reality. The DSM–5 defines psychotic disorders as mental disorders involving one or more of the following: delusions, hallucinations, disorganized thinking, and negative impact of these symptoms on the individual. (DSM–5, at 87).

Delusions are untrue beliefs that the person won't give up despite contrary evidence. Examples include delusions of persecution ("The FBI is after me"), delusions of reference (belief that comments or behaviors of others are directed at the deluded person, "My contracts professor is acting strangely, and his behavior is about me."), delusions of grandeur ("I am a famous movie actor"), and erotomanic delusions ("Matt Damon is in love with me").

The DSM–5 defines hallucinations as "perception-like experiences that occur without an external stimulus. They are vivid and clear, with the full force and impact of normal perceptions, and not under voluntary control." (DSM–5, at 87). There are auditory hallucinations (hearing voices), visual hallucinations (seeing), olfactory (smelling), gustatory (tasting), and tactile (*e.g.*, believing spiders are crawling under one's skin).

Disorganized thinking is referred to as thought disorder, and often is detected in the person's speech. The person may switch suddenly and irrationally between subjects (loose associations). A person's thinking may be so chaotic that speech makes little sense, a condition called word salad.

Individuals suffering from psychosis often have "diminished emotional expression" (DSM–5, at p. 88), sometimes called flat affect, as well as avolition, reduced motivation, and anhedonia, decreased pleasure in life. Many psychotics are depressed. It can be impossible to tell whether diminished emotional expression is a result of depression or psychosis or both.

The DSM–5 lists the following disorders under psychotic disorders: Schizotypal Personality Disorder, Delusional Disorder, Brief Psychotic Disorder, Schizophreniform Disorder, and Schizophrenia. The difference between Schizophreniform Disorder and Schizophrenia is duration. To be diagnosed with schizophrenia, the person must be symptomatic longer than six months.

As many as 3.5 million Americans suffer from schizophrenia. In bygone days, schizophrenia was called dementia precox (premature dementia), in part because the illness often manifests itself in the late teen years or early twenties. The cause (or causes) of schizophrenia is unknown, although evidence increasingly points to chemical issues in the brain. There is a genetic component to the disorder.

Various antipsychotic medications are available, and provide relief to thousands of patients. Yet, many patients resist medication because of the way the medicines make them feel. Persons with mental illness cannot be forced to take medicine unless a judge so orders. Issues of medication compliance pose major issues for patients, family members, mental health and legal professionals, police, judges, and policy makers.

Thousands of individuals with schizophrenia live normal lives, holding down a job, marrying, having kids, and enjoying life. Yet, you only have to walk down a city street to see the terrible impact of this illness. Severe schizophrenia destroys the personality, making normalcy impossible, and causing heartache for patients, their parents, siblings, and extended family. Suicide is common.

Mental health services for the seriously mentally ill are inadequate. A psychotic patient living on the street is more likely to come face-to-face with a police officer than a mental health professional. Although police do their best, they are cops, not counselors. Tragically, our jails are filled with people suffering serious, largely untreated, mental illness.

K.   BIPOLAR AND RELATED DISORDERS

Bipolar Disorder is also known as manic-depressive disorder. The DSM–5 intentionally locates Bipolar Disorder in the pages between schizophrenia, on one hand, and depression, on the other. This placement is designed to emphasize that bipolar bridges schizophrenia and depression "in terms of symptomatology, family history, and genetics." (DSM–5, at p. 123). Bipolar Disorder is sometimes a very serious illness, with significant impact on a person's life.

The DSM–5 recognizes two categories of Bipolar Disorder: Bipolar 1 and Bipolar 2. For a diagnosis of Bipolar 1, the individual must experience at least one manic episode "of abnormally and persistently elevated, expansive or irritable mood and persistently increased goal-directed activity or energy" (DSM–5, at p. 124), plus at least one episode of major depression. A diagnosis of Bipolar 2 requires at least one episode of major depression, plus at least one episode of hypomania. Bipolar 2 does not require a full blown manic episode. Bipolar 1 is more serious.

L.   DEPRESSIVE DISORDERS

We all get "depressed." Maybe you did poorly on an exam or experienced the breakup of a relationship. The normal ups and downs of life must be distinguished from clinical depression, which can be very serious—sometimes life threatening. To receive a diagnosis of depression, the DSM–5 provides that a person must have five or more of the following, lasting at least two weeks: depressed mood most of the day, diminished interest in normal activities, significant weight loss, insomnia or sleeping too much, agitation or lethargy, loss of energy, feelings of worthlessness or guilt, difficulty concentrating, ruminations about death. The symptoms cause significant distress, and interfere with normal functioning.

M.   ANXIETY DISORDERS

According to the DSM–5, "anxiety disorders include disorders that share features of excessive fear and anxiety and related behavioral disturbances." (DSM–5, at p. 189). Anxiety disorders include social anxiety disorder (fear of social situations); panic disorder (recurrent, abrupt attacks of intense fear); agoraphobia (fear of using public transportation, open or enclosed spaces, *e.g.*, theater, being in a crowd, and fear of being outside the home); and generalized anxiety disorder.

N.   OBSESSIVE-COMPULSIVE DISORDERS

Obsessive-Compulsive Disorder (OCD), as the name suggests, is characterized by obsessions and/or compulsions. The DSM–5 states, "Obsessions are recurrent and persistent thoughts, urges, or images that are experienced as intrusive and unwanted, whereas compulsions are repetitive behaviors or mental acts that an individual feels driven to perform in response to an obsession. . . ." (p. 235). Many individuals with OCD also suffer serious anxiety.

Although the obsessions and compulsions seen in OCD vary, it is common to observe obsessive cleaning (*e.g.*, hand washing), preoccupation with symmetry (everything must be in exactly the "right place"), and ritualistic behavior.

Body Dysmorphic Disorder is preoccupation with a perceived flaw in one's appearance.

Hoarding Disorder involves a persistent inability to "throw things away" to the point that the accumulated "stuff" significantly interferes with the person's life (*e.g.*, piles of paper reach the ceiling, making it is difficult to move about the home).

Trichotillomania Disorder is the chronic pulling out of one's own hair.

Excoriation Disorder is chronic skin picking.

O.   TRAUMA-RELATED DISORDERS

The most well-known trauma-related disorder is Posttraumatic Stress Disorder. PTSD is diagnosed in people who experience or witness trauma that threatens death, serious injury, or sexual violence. Because of the trauma, the person experiences some or all of the following: intrusive distressing memories, dreams about the trauma, dissociative reactions (*e.g.*, flashbacks in which the person is back in the traumatic situation), intense distress when something triggers memories of the trauma.

Reactive Attachment Disorder is observed in some babies and young children who experience severe neglect. This form of neglect is also known as Non-Organic Failure to Thrive.

P.   DISSOCIATIVE DISORDERS

The DSM–5 states, "Dissociative Disorders are characterized by a disruption of and/or discontinuity in the normal integration of consciousness, memory, identity, emotion, perception, body representation, motor control, and behavior." Dissociative Identity Disorder, commonly known as multiple personality disorder, is a rare disorder involving two or more distinct personality states.

Q.   SOMATIC DISORDERS

Somatic disorders focus on the body rather than the mind. Thus, in Somatic Symptom Disorder, the patient has excessive thoughts about physical illness. With Illness Anxiety Disorder, the patient is preoccupied with catching a serious illness. Factitious Disorder is the falsification of symptoms. Factitious Disorder Imposed on Another, also known as Munchausen Syndrome by Proxy, is a rare form of child abuse in which an adult causes illness in a child, usually in order to gain attention for the adult.

R. EATING DISORDERS

The eating disorders include Pica (persistent eating of non-food items, *e.g.*, bottle caps); Rumination Disorder (repeatedly throwing up); Restrictive Food Intake Disorder (not eating enough); Anorexia Nervosa (extreme weight loss due to not eating, and intense fear of gaining weight); Bulimia Nervosa (binge eating, often accompanied by self-induced vomiting to avoid gaining weight).

S. PARAPHILIC DISORDERS

The word paraphilia refers to intense sexual interest in matters other than normal sex, however normal is defined. Voyeuristic Disorder involves sexual arousal from spying on someone disrobing or engaged in sexual activity. States have so-called "Peeping Tom" laws to criminalize such behavior. Exhibitionistic Disorder is sexual arousal from exposing oneself. Frotteuristic Disorder is sexual arousal from rubbing up against a non-consenting person. (*See Commonwealth v. Shin*, 86 Mass. App. Ct. 381, 16 N.E.3d 1122 (2014)). Sexual Masochism and Sexual Sadism Disorders require no explanation. Pedophilic Disorder is sexual arousal regarding sex with children. Fetishistic Disorder is sexual arousal to the use of non-living objects, or a focus on specific non-genital body parts (*e.g.*, feet).

T. DEMENTIA AND DELIRIUM

The population of older Americans is growing. By 2030, the number of Americans over 65 will approach 70 million. Among the elderly, the most rapidly growing age group is seniors over 85. Old age and disability are not synonyms. The Tennessee Court of Appeals observed, "The aging process, by itself, is not a disabling condition, and being elderly is not tantamount to being disabled. The popular notion that the aging process entails progressive decline in capacity or competence vastly oversimplifies a complex process that affects an extraordinarily large and diverse group of persons." (*In re Conservatorship of Groves*, 109 S.W.3d 317, 331–332 (Tenn. Ct. App. 2003)). Yet, like a vintage automobile, the aging human body is prone to break down. Reflexes slow, balance becomes precarious, muscle and bone weaken, eyesight deteriorates, hearing falters, memory goes, etc. etc. A healthy lifestyle, especially diet and exercise, can hold aging at bay and improve quality of life. In the end, however, father time has his way.

Two issues of aging raise special concerns for readers of this book—dementia and delirium. The DSM–5 notes, "The prevalence of overall dementia rises steeply with age. In high-income countries, it ranges from 5% to 10% in the seventh decade to at least 25% thereafter.

DEMENTIA

Mario Mendez and Jeffrey Cummings write, "Dementia is a syndrome of acquired intellectual impairment produced by brain dysfunction." (Mario F. Mendez & Jeffrey L. Cummings, *Dementia: A Clinical Approach,* p. 1 (2003)). The DSM–5 uses the term "neurocognitive disorders" to embrace dementia and delirium. The DSM–5 diagnostic criteria for dementia include, "Evidence of significant cognitive decline from a previous level of performance in one or more cognitive domains (complex attention, executive function, learning and memory, language, perceptual-motor, or social cognition) based on . . . a significant decline in cognitive function and a substantial impairment of cognitive performance." (p. 602). The term "senility" was once used to describe dementia. Today, the word "senility" is falling into disuse, as is the term "organic brain syndrome."

The most common cause of dementia in elders is Alzheimer's disease. The onset of Alzheimer's is slow, and involves continuing cognitive decline. Elaine Peskind and Murray Raskind describe the typical course of dementia of the Alzheimer's type (DAT):

> DAT begins insidiously. Subtle difficulties in recent memory are almost always the first sign. Personality changes also occur early and most often are manifested by apathy and loss of interest in persons and activities. Memory impairment gradually becomes more severe and deficits in other cognitive domains, such as executive function and visual-spatial skills, appear. Usually after several years of cognitive impairment, a fluent type of aphasia begins, characterized by difficulty naming objects or choosing the right word to express an idea. Apraxia often occurs con-currently, and the loss of ability to perform often routine motor activities, such as eating with utensils or dressing, can pose tremendous care burdens on

the patient's family and other care providers. In the later stages of DAT, patients develop disturbed sleep/wake cycles, begin to wander, have episodes of irritability and motor hyperactivity, and lose their ability to attend to personal care needs such as dressing, feeding, and personal hygiene. The course of the illness is rarely less than 5 years and may extend to more than 15 years.

Elaine R. Peskind & Murray A. Rashkind, Cognitive Disorders. In Ewald W. Busse & Dan G. Blazer, *Textbook of Geriatric Psychiatry* 213–234, at 218 (2d ed. 1996).

Mario Mendez and Jeffrey Cummings observe that with Alzheimer's, "Not only must families observe the deterioration of their loved ones, but they are often exhausted caring for them and may lose their life savings in the process." (Mario F. Mendez & Jeffrey L. Cummings, *Dementia: A Clinical Approach* 1 (2003)). Depression occurs in 20 to 60 percent of caregivers providing for relatives with dementia.

In addition to Alzheimer's disease, other dementing illnesses are Parkinson's disease and Huntington's disease.

Treatment is nonexistent or limited for some dementias (*e.g.,* Alzheimer's). A number of dementias, can be managed or even reversed. For example, dementia caused by medication is sometimes reversible.

DELIRIUM

Most forms of dementia worsen slowly and are chronic. Delirium, by contrast, is a disturbance of consciousness that generally has a prompt onset measured in hours or days. The DSM–5 diagnostic criteria for delirium state, "The disturbance develops over a short period of time (usually hours to a few days)." (p. 596) Delirium is caused by medical conditions, infections, dehydration, malnutrition, medications, substance abuse, and other causes. Sharon Inouye writes, "Although it can occur in any setting, delirium is most common in settings where the frailty and illness acuity of patients are most severe. The incidence of delirium increases with age, cognitive impairment, frailty, illness severity, comorbidity, and other risk factors for delirium." (Sharon K. Inouye, Delirium. In Christine K. Cassel (Ed.), *Geriatric Medicine: An Evidence-Based Approach* 1113–1121, at 1113 (4th ed. 2003)). Delirium often disappears with treatment, and sometimes on its own. Many patients experience full recovery.

Delirium occurs in people of all ages, although the elderly are especially susceptible. People of any age in the hospital may suffer delirium. The DSM–5 reports, "The prevalence of delirium when individuals are admitted to the hospital ranges from 14% to 24%, and estimates of the incidence of delirium arising during hospitalization range from 6% to 56% in general hospital populations. Delirium occurs in 15%–53% of older individuals postoperatively and in 70%–87% of those in intensive care. Delirium occurs in up to 60% of individuals in nursing homes or post-acute care settings and in up to 83% of all individuals at the end of life." (p. 600).

DECISION-MAKING IN THE ELDERLY

Most older persons are fully competent and autonomous. Yet, aging is sometimes accompanied by illness, injury, or mental impairment that compromises decision-making capacity. The Tennessee Court of Appeals wrote:

> Because of the importance of autonomy, it is well-settled that the law presumes that adult persons are sane, rather than insane, and capable, rather than incapable, to direct their personal affairs until satisfactory evidence to the contrary is presented. Mental or physical impairment should never be presumed. The force of these presumptions does not wane as a person ages. . . .

> Incapacity is the legal status that occurs when a person's autonomy becomes either partially or totally impaired. A person lacks the ability to be autonomous—to exercise free will—when he or she lacks the ability to absorb information, to understand its implications, to correctly perceive the environment, or to understand the relationship between his or her desires and actions. A person is likewise incapacitated when he or she cannot control his or her actions or behavior.

In re Conservatorship of Groves, 109 S.W.3d 317, 328–330 (Tenn. Ct. App. 2003).

Deficits in decision-making capacity can be proven with evidence of the individual's behavior, out-of-court statements, and in-court communication and demeanor. Lay and expert testimony is admissible. Formal psychological assessment often plays a decisive role in determining capacity. Medical and mental health professionals consider the following factors in assessing decision-making capacity: Ability to make a choice; ability to make a reasonable choice; ability to appreciate the implications of a choice; ability to reason; and ability to understand.

When questions arise about an older person's mental functioning, a psychiatric or psychological examination may be necessary. Integral to the examination are the elder's history and current functioning. Current functioning is evaluated by conducting a mental status examination, which assesses disturbances in consciousness, mood, affect, motor functioning, perception (*e.g.*, hallucinations), memory, and intelligence.

In addition to the mental status examination, a number of screening devices are available to assist in assessing mental functioning. Screening devices are not sufficient to reach a diagnosis, but are valuable pieces of the diagnostic puzzle. One generally accepted screening technique for cognitive function is the Mini-Mental State Examination (MMSE). The MMSE has been normed for various ages and levels of education. The professional who administers the MMSE asks the patient a series of questions, including, "What year is this?" and "What town are we in?" Short-term memory is tested by asking the patient to remember and repeat three simple words (ball, car, man). The patient is asked to perform a simple motor task (fold a piece of paper and place it on the floor). Next, the patient is asked to write a complete sentence. Finally, the patient is asked to copy a simple geometric design. Points are given for correct responses. The higher the score, the better.

The Mini-Mental State Examination is mentioned in a number of court decisions. The Tennessee Court of Appeals referred to it as "the instrument most commonly used to assess cognitive competency in adults." (*In re Conservatorship of Groves*, 109 S.W.3d 317, 340 n.99 (Tenn. Ct. App. 2003). *See also, Estate of Rubenstein v. Unites States*, 119 Fed. Cl. 658 (2015) (taxpayer refund claim); *Hooke v. Colvin*, 20 F. Supp. 3d 286 (D. Mass. 2014) (Social Security disability); *Longgrear v. Colvin*, 20 F. Supp. 3d 1066 (D. Colo. 2014) (Social Security disability); *United States v. Gigante*, 996 F. Supp. 194 (E.D.N.Y. 1998); *Connor v. Schlemmer*, 996 A.2d 98 (R.I. 2010) ("Dr. Stoukides testified that Kathleen 'scored 19 out of 30' on the Folstein Mini-Mental State Exam."); *Landmark Trust (USA), Inc. v. Goodhue*, 172 Vt. 515, 782 A.2d 1219 (2001) ("The MMSE is a screening device to determine whether more comprehensive testing of cognitive function is necessary. The test does not permit conclusive assessment of cognitive capabilities.")).

Another frequently used screen is the Short Portable Mental Status Questionnaire (SPMSQ).

Dan Glazer writes, "The SPMSQ consists of 10 questions designed to assess orientation, memory, fund of knowledge, and calculation. For most community-dwelling older adults, two or fewer errors indicates intact functioning; three or more errors, mild impairment; five to seven errors, moderate impairment; and eight or more errors, severe impairment. The ease of administration and the reliability of this instrument, as supported by accumulated epidemiological data, make it useful for both clinical and community screens." (Dan G. Glazer, The Psychiatric Interview of the Geriatric Patient. In Ewald W. Busse & Dan G. Blazer, *Textbook of Geriatric Psychiatry* 175–189, at 182 (2d ed. 1996)).

U.   ADDITIONAL DISORDERS

The DSM–5 contains many additional disorders, including insomnia; hypersomnolence (can't stay awake, *e.g.*, civil procedure class); Narcolepsy (involuntary falling asleep at inappropriate times); Nightmare Disorder, Restless Legs Syndrome (urge to move the legs, often while resting); Oppositional Defiant Disorder (chronic angry mood and defiant behavior); Conduct Disorder (chronic disregard for the rights of others (bullying, initiating fights); Pyromania (fire setting); substance abuse and addiction; Caffine Withdrawal (often observed in law students when final exams are finished); Personality Disorders, including Paranoid Personality Disorder, Schizoid Personality Disorder (pattern of detachment from social relationships, accompanied by limited emotions);   Antisocial   Personality   Disorder;

Borderline Personality Disorder (chronic instability of relationships with others, impulsivity, difficulties with self-image and affect); Histrionic Personality Disorder (excessive attention getting behavior and emotionality); Narcissistic Personality Disorder (excessive self-centeredness and feelings of superiority).

The World Health Organization publishes the International Classification of Diseases, now in its tenth edition, known as ICD–10. The ICD–10 Classification of Mental and Behavioral Disorders parallels the DSM–5 diagnostic categories. The DSM–5 is "harmonized" with the ICD–10. (DSM–5, p. xli).

V.   PSYCHIATRIC MEDICATION

Many individuals with mental disability benefit from medication. The National Institute of Mental Health publishes an online description of mental health medications, which states in part:

> Psychiatric medications treat the symptoms of mental disorders. Sometimes called psychotropic or psychotherapeutic medications, they have changed the lives of people with mental disorders for the better. Many people with mental disorders live fulfilling lives with the help of these medications. Without them, people with mental disorders might suffer serious and disabling symptoms.
>
> Medications work differently for different people. Some people get great results from

medications and only need them for a short time. For example, a person with depression may feel much better after taking medication for a few months, and may never need it again. People with disorders like schizophrenia or bipolar disorder, or people who have long-term or severe depression or anxiety may need to take medication for a much longer time.

The National Institute of Mental Health, *Mental Health Medications* (accessed 6/24/2015).

W. COMPETENCY

The concept of competency pervades civil and criminal law. Thus, witnesses must be competent to testify, a testator must be competent to make a will (testamentary capacity), a criminal defendant must be competent to stand trial, children generally lack competence to consent to medical procedures, etc. etc. The legal and psychological elements of competency vary from context to context. In 1977, Loren Roth and his colleagues observed that the search for a single theory of competence is a "search for a holy grail." (Loren H. Roth, et al., Tests for Competency to Consent to Treatment, 134 *American Journal of Psychiatry* 279, at p. 283 (1977)). In 2008, Michael Perlin and his colleagues noted that the decades intervening since Roth's observation "have underscored the prescience and continued vitality of this observation. Developments in every relevant area of the law—criminal law, mental disability law, private law—have yielded multiple definitions and meanings of 'competency.' . . . [H]undreds of reported appellate cases each year explore the meaning of the term 'competency' in cases involving, variously, a criminal defendant's right to waive counsel, a psychiatric patient's right to sexual interaction, a testator's right to bequeath money as she sees fit, a hospital patient's right to consent to experimental treatment, the right of institutionalized civil psychiatric patients to make autonomous treatment decisions, the right of a currently incompetent-to-stand-trial jail detainee to refuse medication that would make him competent to be tried, or the right to decide to marry. And this short list barely scratches the surface." (Michael L. Perlin, Pamela Champine, Henry A. Dlugacz & Mary Connell, *Competence in the Law: From Legal Theory to Clinical Application,* pp. 1–2 (2008)).

X. REPRESENTING MENTALLY ILL CLIENTS

Representing mentally ill and intellectually disabled clients is enormously rewarding because lawyers provide concrete assistance that improves lives. Yet, representing individuals with serious mental disorders is challenging. How do you communicate with a client who is hallucinating? Is a client with dementia competent to execute a will, deed, codicil, or other legal document? How do you take direction from a client who won't talk to you because the client is too depressed to speak?

Experience will provide you tools to work effectively with mentally disabled clients, although it must be said that all the experience in the world can't solve the plethora of ethical challenges that will come your way. Ethics codes offer a little help. The *Model Rules of Professional Conduct* (Rule 1.14) speak to the issue:

(a) When a client's capacity to make adequately considered decisions in connection with a representation is diminished, whether because of minority, mental impairment or for some other reason, the lawyer shall, as far as reasonably possible, maintain a normal client-lawyer relationship with the client.

(b) When the lawyer reasonably believes that the client has diminished capacity, is at risk of substantial physical, financial or other harm unless action is taken and cannot adequately act in the client's own interest, the lawyer may take reasonably necessary protective action, including consulting with individuals or entities that have the ability to take action to protect the client and, in appropriate cases, seeking appointment of a guardian ad litem, conservator or guardian.

(c) Information relating to the representation of a client with diminished capacity is protected by Rule 1.6 [confidentiality]. When taking protective action pursuant to paragraph (b), the lawyer is impliedly authorized under Rule 1.6(a) to reveal information about the client, but only to the extent reasonably necessary to protect the client's interests.

The commentary to Rule 1.14 provides useful advice on assessing competence: "In determining the extent of the client's diminished capacity, the lawyer should consider and balance such factors as: the client's ability to articulate reasoning leading to a decision, variability of state of mind and ability to appreciate consequences of a decision; the substantive fairness of a decision; and the consistency of a decision with the known long-term commitments and values of the client. In appropriate circumstances, the lawyer may seek guidance from an appropriate diagnostician."

See Raymond C. O'Brien, Attorney Responsibility and Client Incapacity, 30 *Journal of Contemporary Health Law and Policy* 59 (2013).

CHAPTER 2
CONFIDENTIALITY

Successful relationships between professionals and clients require confidentiality. The American Medical Association (AMA) emphasizes the importance of confidentiality in the physician-patient relationship: "The information disclosed to a physician by a patient should be held in confidence. The patient should feel free to make a full disclosure with the knowledge that the physician will respect the confidential nature of the communication. The physician should not reveal confidential information without the express consent of the patient, subject to certain exceptions which are ethically justified because of overriding considerations." (AMA Ethics Opinion 5.05—Confidentiality (2007)).

The importance of confidentiality is equally applicable to mental health and legal professionals. Ask yourself, if you seek help from a psychotherapist, will you reveal your deepest secrets if you know the therapist is free to discuss your case on the six o'clock news? If a teenage girl wants birth control, might she cancel her appointment if she learns the doctor will call her parents? If Samantha is charged with a crime, will she feel safe telling you, her lawyer, *all* the details, if she believes police can compel you to repeat what she said in the privacy of your office? Without confidentiality, professional relationships are nipped in the bud. By contrast, when professionals promise confidentiality, relationships blossom in an atmosphere of trust. Confidentiality is indispensable for success in the helping professions.

A. CONFIDENTIALITY DEFINED

The dictionary defines confidentiality as "private" or "secret." The federal Health Insurance Portability and Accountability Act (HIPAA) plays an important role in defining and enforcing confidentiality. The HIPAA Privacy Rule defines confidentiality as follows: "Confidentiality means the property that data or information is not made available or disclosed to unauthorized persons or processes" (Code of Federal Regulations, Title 45, § 164.304) (HIPAA is discussed later in this chapter).

There are five primary sources of confidentiality. First, there is the commonsense idea that some information is private. You don't need laws to tell you certain information should not see the light of day. Second, the ethics codes of professional organizations emphasize confidentiality. Third, every state and the federal government have complex laws governing confidentiality (*e.g.*, HIPAA Privacy Rule). Fourth, in legal proceedings, confidential communications between clients and certain professionals are protected from disclosure by evidentiary privileges such as the psychotherapist-client privilege and the physician-patient privilege. Fifth, clients have privacy rights guaranteed by the constitution.

B. ETHICS CODES

The ethics codes of the helping professions focus a great deal of attention on confidentiality. For example, the American Psychological Association's *Ethical Principles of Psychologists and Code of Conduct* (APA *Code of Conduct*) states,

"Psychologists respect the dignity and worth of all people, and the rights of individuals to privacy, confidentiality, and self-determination." (General Principle E). The APA *Code of Conduct* states that psychologists have a "primary obligation to take reasonable precautions to protect confidential information." (Ethical Standard 4.01).

The National Association of Social Workers' *Code of Ethics* (NASW *Code of Ethics*) provides, "Social workers should respect clients' right to privacy.... Social workers should protect the confidentiality of all information obtained in the course of professional service." (Ethical Standard 1.07(a) and (c)).

The *Code of Ethics for Nurses* of the American Nurses Association provides, "The nurse has a duty to maintain confidentiality of all patient information." (Provision 3.2).

Medical students take the Hippocratic Oath, written in the fifth century B.C. by the father of medicine, Hippocrates (or one of his students). The original oath provided, "Whatever, in the course of my practice, I may see or hear ..., whatever I may happen to obtain knowledge of, if it be not proper to repeat it, I will keep sacred and secret...." Hippocrates lives on in today's *Code of Medical Ethics,* quoted at the beginning of this chapter.

Lawyers share the commitment to confidentiality. The American Bar Association's *Model Rules of Professional Conduct* state, "A lawyer shall not reveal information relating to the representation of a client...." (Rule 1.6(a)). California law emphasizes the lawyer's duty to protect confidential information: "It is the duty of an attorney to . . . maintain inviolate the confidence, and at every peril to himself or herself to preserve the secrets of his or her client." (Cal. Business and Professions Code § 6068(e)(1)).

C. CONSTITUTIONAL PRIVACY

The U.S. Constitution does not mention a right of privacy or confidentiality. In decisions spanning more than a century, however, the U.S. Supreme Court has interpreted the Constitution to guarantee citizens a limited right to privacy vis-a-vie the government. Thus, in 1973, the High Court predicated a woman's right to abortion on privacy (*Roe v. Wade,* 410 U.S. 113, 93 S. Ct. 705 (1973)).

Five state constitutions—Alaska, California, Florida, Hawai'i, and Montana—expressly mention a right to privacy. Florida's Constitution provides, "Every natural person has the right to be let alone and from governmental intrusion into the person's private life. . . ." (Florida Constitution Art., 1, § 23). The California Constitution states, "All people are by nature free and independent and have inalienable rights. Among these are enjoying and defending . . . privacy." (California Constitution, Art. 1, § 1). Although constitutions in most states don't specifically mention privacy, judges interpret state constitutions to protect privacy.

D. FEDERAL AND STATE LAWS ON CONFIDENTIALITY—HIPAA

Every state has complex laws governing confidentiality of records. Any effort to describe the specifics of confidentiality law in all 50 states would take a thousand of pages, would be immediately out of date, and would put you to sleep. There is one law, however, a federal regulation called the HIPAA Privacy Rule, which has such a pervasive impact across the country that it is worth studying in some detail (*See* Code of Federal Regulations, Title 45, Part 164).

The HIPAA Privacy Rule protects the confidentiality of health and mental health information. The Rule is broad, protecting all "individually identifiable health information." HIPAA applies to most health and mental health professionals in the United States. Professionals and entities covered by HIPAA are called "covered entities." The Privacy Rule requires covered professionals to ensure the confidentiality, integrity, and availability of all electronic health information. In addition, professionals must take reasonable steps to protect against threats to the security of electronically stored health information (*e.g.*, protections against hacking).

The Privacy Rule is too complex to describe in detail. The highlights are summarized below.

Consultation and Training. HIPAA respects the time-honored tradition of professionals consulting each other about cases. HIPAA understands that supervisors discuss cases with trainees. (45 C.F.R. § 164.506(a)).

Client Access. Clients have the right to inspect and copy their health information (45 C.F.R. § 164.502(a)(2)). A "personal representative" is a person who is legally authorized to make health care decisions for a client. If a client has a personal representative, the representative has the right to inspect and copy health information.

Client May Authorize Disclosure. Professionals cannot disclose protected health information without proper authorization (45 C.F.R. § 164.508(a)). Clients may authorize the release of health information covered by HIPAA. Professionals may obtain client consent to use or disclose health information in order to carry out treatment and to obtain payment (45 C.F.R. § 164.506(b)).

Disclose the Minimum. When professionals disclose health information, HIPAA requires release of the minimum amount of information needed to accomplish the purpose of the release.

Requirements for Valid Authorization to Disclose. To be valid, an authorization for disclosure must: (1) Describe the information to be disclosed; (2) State who is authorized to disclose; (3) State to whom disclosure is authorized; (4) Describe the purpose of the disclosure ("At the request of the individual" will suffice); (5) Specify the date, or an event, when authorization ends; (6) Contain the signature and date by the person authorizing disclosure; (7) Contain a statement that the client can revoke the authorization; (8) Be written in plain language; (9) The client must be given a copy of the signed authorization.

Client Can Revoke Authorization. A client can revoke authorization to disclose health information (45 C.F.R. § 164.508(b)(iii) and (5)).

HIPAA Rule on Children and Adolescents. As a general matter, parents have the right to inspect their child's health records, communicate with professionals about their child's care, and authorize release of their child's health information (45 C.F.R. § 164.502(g)(3)(i)).

When it comes to adolescents, things get tricky. In a legal sense, a teenager is still a "child." Thus, parents can talk to professionals treating the "child." At the same time, state laws allow teenagers to consent to certain medical and mental health care, without parental involvement. When these laws apply, HIPAA specifies that parents do not have the right to a teenager's medical information (45 C.F.R. § 164.502(g)(3)(i)(A) and (B)).

HIPAA gives licensed health care professionals authority to exercise judgment to decide, in individual cases, that parents should be denied access to a child's health care information (45 C.F.R. § 164.502(g)(3)(ii)(C)). A professional may deny parental access to their child's medical record when the professional reasonably believes a parent has neglected or abused the child, or when allowing parental access could endanger the child, and allowing access is not in the child's best interest. (45 C.F.R. § 164.502(g)(5)(i)(A), (B), (ii)).

HIPAA specifies that parents can sign "an agreement of confidentiality," in which parents agree to respect the confidentiality of communications between a professional and their child. (45 C.F.R. § 164.502(g)(3)(i)(C)). In practice, most mental health professionals who work with children—particularly adolescents—insist that parents respect the privacy of communications between the therapist and the child.

Rule for Psychotherapy Notes. The HIPAA Privacy Rule has special protections for psychotherapy notes, which the Rule defines as notes (recorded in any medium) recorded by mental health professionals documenting or analyzing the contents of conversations during private therapy sessions, group sessions, or joint or family therapy, "that are separated from the rest of the individual's medical record." (45 C.F.R. § 164.502). "Psychotherapy notes" does not include "medication prescription and monitoring, counseling session start and stop times, the modalities and frequencies of treatment furnished, results of clinical tests, and any summary of the following items: Diagnosis, functional status, the treatment plan, symptoms, prognosis, and progress to date." (45 C.F.R. § 164.501).

Some mental health professionals organize client files to keep "psychotherapy notes" in separate files. Doing so surrounds this highly sensitive information with added protection from disclosure. For example, insurance plans cannot demand access to psychotherapy notes.

Disclosure of psychotherapy notes requires a separate release, signed by the client (45 C.F.R. § 164.508(a)(2)). A separate release is not required to use psychotherapy notes for training and supervision (45 C.F.R. § 164.508(2)(i)(B)).

Disclosures for judicial proceedings. A professional may release health information in response to a court order. (45 C.F.R. § 164.512(e)). As well, release is permitted in response to a subpoena or discovery request, so long as the party seeking release meets certain requirements. (45 C.F.R. § 164.512(e)).

Most courts hold HIPAA does not forbid ex parte contact with treating professionals. A person (*e.g.*, an attorney) may contact a patient's health care provider. Of course, HIPAA and other laws limit what, if anything, the provider may say. In *Caldwell v. Chauvin*, 464 S.W.3d 139 (Ky. 2015), the Kentucky Supreme Court wrote, "[W]e conclude that no law inhibits litigants from seeking ex parte interviews with the opposing party's treating physicians. But the disclosure of medical information during those ex parte meetings is controlled by HIPAA. For disclosure to be permitted, the party must first obtain a court order authorizing disclosure in a voluntary ex parte interview."

Federal law provides added confidentiality for patient records of alcohol and drug abuse treatment in "any federally assisted alcohol and drug abuse program." (42 C.F.R. § 2.3(a)). It is a crime to improperly disclose such records. (42 C.F.R. § 2.4). It violates the law even to disclose that a person is a patient. (42 C.F.R. § 2.13(c)). The client may consent to release of patient information. (42 C.F.R. § 2.31). The law allows reports of suspected child abuse. (42 C.F.R. § 2.12(c)(6)). A court may order disclosure of records. Information may be disclosed in emergencies.

E. PRIVILEGE

This section discusses evidentiary privileges. The word "evidentiary" is used because privilege law is part of the law of evidence. Evidentiary privileges apply only in legal proceedings. Five evidentiary privileges are described: psychotherapist-client privilege; physician-patient privilege; attorney-client privilege; clergy-penitent privilege; and spousal privileges. Nearly all states have these privileges, and some states have more. California, for example, adds a sexual assault counselor-victim privilege (California Evidence Code § 1035.8) and a domestic violence counselor-client privilege (California Evidence Code § 1037.5).

In *People v. Rivera*, 25 N.Y.3d 256 (2015), the New York Court of Appeals described the benefits of privileges:

The privilege serves several objectives: it encourages unrestrained communication between a patient and his or her medical provider so that the patient may obtain diagnosis and treatment without fear of embarrassment over potential disclosure; it encourages physicians to be forthright in recording their patients' confidential information; and it protects patients' reasonable privacy expectations against disclosure of sensitive personal information. 25 N.Y.3d at 261.

With the exception of the spousal privileges, the privileges analyzed here share the same elements: (1) a client or patient; (2) a professional who is covered by privilege law; (3) communication between the client/patient and the professional; and (4) an expectation that the communication will not be disclosed.

Evidentiary privileges are close kin of ethical duties of confidentiality. Both spring from the importance of privacy in professional relationships. How do they differ? First, evidentiary privileges apply only in legal proceedings. By contrast, ethical duties of confidentiality apply everywhere—at the office, a restaurant, a professional conference, *and* in legal proceedings.

An example illustrates the distinction between evidentiary privilege and the ethical duty of confidentiality. Sarah is a clinical social worker in private practice. Sarah has an ethical duty to protect confidential client information. As well, Sarah is a psychotherapist covered by her state's psychotherapist-client privilege. Sarah is treating Beth for depression. After work, Sarah and her friend, Ruth, are enjoying a meal. During dinner, is Sarah free to discuss Beth's case with her friend? Of course not. Does the prohibition arise from the ethical duty? The psychotherapist-client privilege? Both? The answer is, Sarah's duty to maintain confidentiality over dinner is based on her ethical duty, and has nothing to do with privilege. Evidentiary privileges apply in legal proceedings, not over salad.

What is a "legal proceeding" for purposes of privilege? Clearly, proceedings in court (*e.g.*, testimony) are "legal proceedings." In addition, a pretrial deposition is a legal proceeding. A subpoena that requests production of privileged records occurs in a legal proceeding.

A second difference between privilege and ethical duty is breadth of coverage. The ethical duty covers all information on a client, including administrative information about the client, as well as communications during therapy. Privileges apply only to confidential communications in the course of a professional relationship. It should be added that a number of courts hold that the patient's name is privileged.

A third distinction between privilege and ethical duty is that in legal proceedings, privileged communications have greater protection from disclosure than information covered by the ethical duty of confidentiality. For example, a subpoena overrides the ethical duty of confidentiality, but not a privilege. So too in court: When a professional testifies, a question that requires disclosure of ethically protected information must be answered. By contrast, a question that would require revelation

of privileged information does not have to be
answered.

F.   PSYCHOTHERAPIST-CLIENT PRIVILEGE

All states and federal courts have some version of
the psychotherapist-client privilege. The privilege
protects confidential communications between
clients and therapists from disclosure in legal
proceedings. The privilege applies in all legal
proceedings, civil, criminal, and administrative.
Communications remain privileged after the
therapeutic relationship ends, and the privilege
continues after the client dies.

The privilege belongs to the client, not the
therapist—the client is the holder of the privilege.
Although the client is the holder of the privilege, the
therapist is ethically (and in some states, legally)
obliged to assert the privilege whenever privileged
information is sought.

When a therapist believes a person or an agency
(*e.g.*, prosecutor) is seeking access to privileged
information, the therapist should first consult the
client. A competent client may authorize access to
privileged information. The therapist should inform
the client that once privileged information is
disclosed, the privilege generally no longer applies.
The professional should discuss with the client the
pros and cons of releasing privileged information.
Most clients have little understanding of the
protection afforded by privilege. If the client wants a
privilege respected, the professional should consult
an attorney.

A subpoena does *not* override the psychotherapist-client privilege. Mental health and medical professionals need to understand that although a subpoena should not be ignored, not all subpoenas are valid. A subpoena that is invalid, or that seeks privileged communications, can be quashed by filing a motion to quash. (*See State ex rel. Phillips v. Hackett*, 469 S.W.3d 506 (Mo. Ct. App. 2015) (a party cannot obtain privileged matters through pretrial discovery).

Although a subpoena should not be ignored, a mental health professional can get in trouble for *obeying* a subpoena! Consider Polly Rost, a psychologist. Rost supervised a trainee providing therapy to a child. The child had recurring headaches from a fall at a community center. The child's mother sued the community center. The attorney for the community center sent a subpoena to Rost for the child's treatment records. Rost sent the records. Although the mother had previously authorized release of records to the child's attorney, there was no permission to release records to the community center or its attorney. Rost did not contact the mother or her attorney for permission to release the records. Rost was officially reprimanded for disclosing confidential records without proper authorization. The court reviewing the reprimand wrote, "Rost had a duty to either obtain written permission to release the records from [the child's parent] or challenge the propriety of the subpoena before a judge. Rost did neither. Instead, she unilaterally gave [the child's] records to [the community center attorney] without consulting with [the child's parent] or [the parent's] attorney. Since the language of [the governing ethical principles] unambiguously prohibits this type of conduct," the court approved the reprimand. Thus, Polly Rost got in trouble for complying with a subpoena! (*Rost v. State Board of Psychology*, 659 A.2d 626 (Pa. Commonwealth Court 1995)).

G.   PHYSICIAN-PATIENT PRIVILEGE

Most states have a physician-patient privilege. The U.S. Supreme Court has not approved the physician-patient privilege for federal criminal trials.

The patient is the holder of the physician-patient privilege. As is true of the psychotherapist-client privilege, a physician is ethically (and in some states legally) obliged to assert the privilege on behalf of the patient.

The physician-patient privilege covers confidential communications between doctor and patient. Also within the privilege is information the doctor observes while examining a patient. (*Cole v. Panos*, 128 A.D.3d 880, 11 N.Y.S.3d 179 (2015)).

In some states, the physician-patient privilege does not apply in criminal cases. By contrast, the psychotherapist-client privilege does apply in criminal litigation. A few states have a nurse-patient privilege.

H.   ATTORNEY-CLIENT PRIVILEGE

The attorney-client privilege is the oldest evidentiary privilege. The client is the holder of the privilege.

Mental health and medical professionals are covered by the *attorney-client* privilege when the mental health or medical professional is hired or court-appointed to assist an attorney prepare for trial. (*Manuel v. State*, 162 So. 3d 1157 (Fla. Ct. App. 2015); *Neuman v. State*, 773 S.E.2d 716 (Ga. 2015)). The California Court of Appeal observed in *Elija W. v. Superior Court*, 216 Cal. App. 4th 140, 153 (2013), "When a psychotherapist is appointed [by a judge] to assist defense counsel, he or she is obligated to maintain the confidentiality of the client's communications not only by the psychotherapist-client privilege but also by the lawyer-client privilege."

I.   SPOUSAL PRIVILEGES

States have two spousal privileges: (1) Spousal testimonial privilege, and (2) Spousal confidential communications privilege.

Under the testimonial privilege, one spouse can refuse to testify against the other. For example, if wife is accused of bank robbery, her husband can refuse to testify against her. The prosecutor cannot force the husband to take the witness stand and testify against his spouse. (*Trammel v. United States*, 445 U.S. 40, 100 S. Ct. 906 (1980)).

Under the testimonial privilege, a spouse *may* testify against their spouse if they wish, but they cannot be forced to testify. Thus, if husband is willing to testify against his wife at her bank robbery trial, he may do so, and wife cannot prevent him from taking the witness stand.

The confidential communications privilege protects private communications between spouses, and is similar, in this respect, to the other privileges discussed here. To continue with the bank robbery case, if husband is willing to testify against his wife, he can take the witness stand, but wife can assert the confidential communications privilege to keep him from revealing private conversations between them.

An important exception to the confidential communications privilege relates to domestic violence and child abuse. Generally, when one spouse is prosecuted for domestic violence or child abuse, the privilege does not apply. (*See People v. Szabo,* 846 N.W.2d 412 (Mich. Ct. App. 2013); *State v. Chenoweth*, 354 P.3d 13 (Wash. Ct. App. 2015)).

J. CLERGY-PENITENT PRIVILEGE

Most states have a clergy-penitent privilege for confidential communications between religious leaders and persons seeking spiritual guidance. (*United States v. Durham*, 93 F. Supp. 3d 1291 (W.D. Okla. 2015)). The Catholic confessional is the most well-known example.

The privilege does not apply to every communication with a member of the clergy. There must be a spiritual component to the communication. (*Commonwealth v. Hunter*, 87 Mass. App. Ct. 260, 28 N.E.3d 1 (2015)).

K. CHILD AS CLIENT

The psychotherapist-client and other privileges apply when the client is a child. Normally, a child's parents assert the child's privilege. (*L.A.N. v. L.M.B.,* 292 P.3d 942 (Colo. 2013)). When a conflict exists between parents and child, however, another adult decides issues related to privilege. In *L.A.N. v. L.M.B.,* 292 P.3d 942 (Colo. 2013), the Colorado Supreme Court ruled that in juvenile court proceedings involving young children, the child's guardian ad litem holds the child's privilege. In California juvenile court proceedings, an abused or neglected child's court-appointed attorney co-holds privileges with the child. (Cal. Welfare & Institutions Code § 317).

L. WAIVER

A privilege can be waived by failing to assert it. Generally, voluntary disclosure of privileged information to outsiders waives privilege. (*Commonwealth v. T.J.W. Jr.,* 114 A.3d 1098 (Pa. Super. 2015)). It is possible, however, to disclose confidential and/or privileged information for limited purposes, and such disclosure is not a general waiver. (*Norskog v. Pfiel,* 197 Ill. 2d 60, 755 N.E.2d 1, 257 Ill. Dec. 899 (2001)).

M. PATIENT-LITIGANT EXCEPTION

When a patient or client sues someone, and seeks to recover damages for physical or mental injury, the defendant has a right to prove that the defendant did not cause the injuries. (*Commonwealth v. T.J.W.,* Jr.

114 A.3d 1098 (Pa. Super. 2015)). The defendant may seek access to the plaintiff's confidential/privileged medical or psychological records to prove that the plaintiff's injuries pre-existed the incident that forms the basis of the law suit (*e.g.*, car accident). The patient-litigant exception to confidentiality and privilege states that when a person intentionally puts their physical and/or mental condition in issue in a law suit by seeking money from a defendant, the defendant may have a right to access records. The plaintiff's decision to sue forfeits the claim to privacy.

See Mitchell v. Eighth Judicial District Court, 348 P.3d 675 (Nev. 2015); *Fagen v. Grand View University*, 861 N.W.2d 825 (Iowa 2015) (describing protocol to balance patient's privacy interests against need for discovery); *Gormley v. Edgar,* 995 A.2d 1197 (Pa. Super. 2010); *In re Termination of Parental Rights of N.G.,* 868 N.W.2d 200 (Wis. Ct. App. 2015) (unpublished disposition) (in termination of parental rights case, parent who relied on her mental records could not claim the records were privileged); Helen A. Anderson, The Psychotherapist Privilege: Privacy and "Garden Variety" Emotional Distress, 21 *George Mason Law Review* 117–156 (2013).

The law in many states provides that the defendant cannot be the one to trigger the patient-litigant exception by putting the plaintiff's mental or physical condition in issue. The initiative must come from the plaintiff. In *Koch v. Cox*, 489 F.3d 384 (D.C. Cir. 2007), for example, the court wrote, "A plaintiff does not put his mental state in issue merely by acknowledging he suffers from depression, for which he is not seeking recompense; nor may a defendant overcome the privilege by putting the plaintiff's mental state in issue." At the same time, however, when a party's mental or physical condition is central to the outcome of a case, the law generally allows judges to balance the need for relevant information against the harm caused by disclosure of confidential information. (*See Mitchell v. Eighth Judicial District Court,* 348 P.3d 675 (Nev. 2015)).

The patient-litigant exception sometimes comes up in contested child custody litigation. One parent seeks the other parent's mental health records in an effort to persuade the judge that the children will be harmed by the parent's mental problems. Courts generally are unsympathetic to this argument, holding that a decision to fight for custody does not place a parent's mental condition in issue. (*See Manela v. Superior Court,* 177 Cal. App. 4th 1139 (2009); *Kinsella v. Kinsella,* 150 N.J. 276, 696 A.2d 556 (1997); *M.M. v. L.M.,* 55 A.3d 1167 (Pa. Super. 2012)). In an appropriate case, a judge may find it necessary to balance a parent's desire to maintain the confidentiality of psychological information against the need to ensure children are safe.

N.   COMPLAINT AGAINST PROFESSIONAL

Suing a professional for malpractice, or filing an ethics complaint against a professional, waives confidentiality and privilege to the extent necessary to allow the professional to defend against the claims. (*Koch v. Cox,* 489 F.3d 384 (D.C. Cir. 2007)).

O. DANGEROUS PATIENT

When a psychotherapist believes a client poses a danger to others or herself, the law allows the therapist to reveal privileged communications to protect the client or others. (*See Walden Behavioral Care v. K.I.*, 471 Mass. 150, 27 N.E.3d 1244 (2015)). California law, for example, states, "There is no [psychotherapist-client privilege] if the psychotherapist has reasonable cause to believe that the patient is in such mental or emotional condition as to be dangerous to himself or to the person or property of another and that disclosure of the communication is necessary to prevent the threatened danger." (Cal. Evid. Code § 1024).

Liability for failing to warn third parties of a dangerous patient—*Tarasoff*—is discussed in Chapter 6.

P. REPORTING LAWS

Laws that require professionals to report suspected child abuse, elder abuse, and other matters override confidentiality and privilege. Reporting laws are discussed later in this chapter.

Q. COURT ORDERED EVALUATION

When a judge orders a person evaluated by a mental health professional, and the professional is asked to prepare a report for the court, expectations of confidentiality differ markedly from psychotherapy. With court-ordered evaluation, privileges typically do not apply; there is reduced or no expectation of confidentiality.

The forensic evaluator discusses the limits of confidentiality with the client. (*See* American Psychological Association, Specialty Guidelines for Forensic Psychology, 68 *American Psychologist* 7–19 (2013) (Guideline 6.01)). The American Academy of Psychiatry and the Law's *Ethics Guidelines for the Practice of Forensic Psychiatry* (2005), provide, "Respect for the individual's right of privacy and the maintenance of confidentiality should be major concerns when performing forensic evaluations. Psychiatrists should maintain confidentiality to the extent possible, given the legal context. Special attention should be paid to the evaluee's understanding of medical confidentiality. A forensic evaluation requires notice to the evaluee and to collateral sources of reasonably anticipated limitations on confidentiality." The Academy recommends informing clients that the professional is not the client's "doctor" or "therapist."

Courts sometimes order people to participate in counseling or psychotherapy. For example, psychotherapy may be a condition of probation. In juvenile court, parents who maltreat children may be ordered into treatment. When therapy (as opposed to forensic evaluation) is court-ordered, the psychotherapist-client privilege generally applies. The California Supreme Court observed in *People v. Gonzales* 56 Cal. 4th 353, 296 P.3d 945 (2013) that, although the privilege applies, a therapist may provide the court with general, nonintrusive information, such as whether the client regularly attends and participates in therapy sessions.

R.   GROUP THERAPY

Therapists are ethically obliged to protect confidentiality. Clients are not. This creates issues in couples, group, and family therapy. Therapists explain the importance of confidentiality, and encourage family and group members to respect the privacy of the group. Gerald Koocher and Jessica Daniel offer this advice, "[G]roup leaders cannot unconditionally promise group members confidentiality. . . . [I]t is important to remind group members frequently about the importance of confidentiality, not just at the beginning of the group." (Gerald P. Koocher & Jessica H. Daniel, Treating Children and Adolescents. In Samuel J. Knapp, Michael G. Gottlieb, Mitchell M. Handlesman & Leon D. VandeCreek (Eds.), *APA Handbook of Ethics in Psychology*, vol. 2, p. 35 (2012)).

The psychotherapist-client privilege applies in couples, group, and family therapy. Normally, when a third person who is not a client is present during therapy, communications are not privileged. Courts generally agree, however, that members of couples, group, and family therapy are not "third persons" for this purpose. (*Farrell L. v. Superior Court*, 203 Cal. App. 3d 521 (1988)). The Minnesota Supreme Court observed in *State v. Andring*, 342 N.W.2d 128 (Minn. 1984):

[W]e conclude that the medical privilege must be construed to encompass statements made in group psychotherapy. The participants in group psychotherapy are not casual third persons who are strangers to the psychiatrist/psychologist/nurse-patient relationship. Rather, every participant has such a relationship with the attending professional, and, in the group therapy setting, the participants actually become part of the diagnostic and therapeutic process for co-participants. . . .

An interpretation which excluded group therapy from the scope of the psychotherapist-patient privilege would seriously limit the effectiveness of group psychotherapy as a therapeutic device. This would be particularly unfortunate because group therapy is a cost-effective method of psychotherapy in that it allows the therapist to treat a number of patients at the same time. It is also more effective with some patients, who, upon hearing other people reveal their innermost thoughts, are less reluctant to reveal their own . . . Because the confidentiality of communications made during group therapy is essential in maintaining its effectiveness as a therapeutic tool, . . . [w]e hold that the scope of the physician-patient medical privilege extends to include confidential group psychotherapy sessions where such sessions are an integral and necessary part of a patient's diagnosis and treatment. (p. 133).

The next section summarizes law and practice governing disclosure of confidential and privileged information.

S. CLIENT AUTHORIZATION

A competent adult client can authorize release of confidential or privileged information. The APA *Code of Ethics* provides, "Psychologists may disclose confidential information with the appropriate consent of the ... individual client/patient ..., unless prohibited by law." (Standard 4.05(a)). In a similar vein, the NASW *Code of Ethics* states, "Social workers may disclose confidential information when appropriate with valid consent from a client or a person legally authorized to consent on behalf of a client" (§ 1.07(b)).

Unauthorized disclosure of confidential or privileged information can result in discipline. *See* Chapter 6. (*See Seider v. Board of Examiners of Psychologists*, 762 A.2d 551 (Maine 2000); *Mississippi State Board of Psychological Examiners v. Hosford*, 508 So. 2d 1049 (Miss. 1987)).

In *Sugarman v. Board of Registration in Medicine*, 422 Mass. 338, 662 N.E.2d 1020 (1996), Dr. Sugarman was retained by a mother in a high conflict custody case with allegations of sexual abuse by the father. The judge imposed a gag order. Dr. Sugarman violated the order by releasing a psychological evaluation and holding a press conference. In upholding discipline, the Massachusetts Supreme Judicial Court found that the doctor undermined public confidence in the integrity of the medical profession. The doctor's conduct violated the family's privacy and her ethical duties as a psychiatrist. The doctor was also wrong to opine about a person she had not evaluated.

T.   DISCLOSE THE MINIMUM NECESSARY

When a professional discloses confidential information—with client consent, or because the law requires disclosure—the professional should disclose only so much as is dictated by the situation. The NASW *Code of Ethics* puts it this way, "In all instances, social workers should disclose the least amount of confidential information necessary to achieve the desired purpose; only information that is directly relevant to the purpose for which the disclosure is made should be revealed" (Ethical Standard 1.07(c)).

U.   DISCLOSURE REQUIRED BY LAW

A professional may release confidential information when the law requires disclosure. An ethics opinion from the American Medical Association states, "When the disclosure of confidential information is required by law or court order, physicians generally notify the patient. Physicians should disclose the minimal information required by law, advocate for the protection of confidential information, and, if appropriate, seek a change in the law." (*See* HIPAA, 45 C.F.R. § 164.512(a)).

V. REPORTING LAWS

Every state has laws requiring professionals to report suspected child maltreatment to child protective services or law enforcement. Most states have similar laws requiring reports of elder abuse and neglect. Doctors are required to report certain wounds. Reporting laws override confidentiality and privilege. (*State v. Strauch,* 345 P.3d 317 (N.M. 2015); *State v. Hyder,* 159 Wash. App. 234, 244 P.3d 454 (2011)). The HIPAA Privacy Rule specifies that professionals may disclose protected health information in order to comply with the duty to report suspected maltreatment. (45 C.F.R. § 164.512(b)(ii)).

In addition to disclosures mandated by reporting laws, HIPAA allows disclosure of health information on victims when disclosure is required by law, the victim agrees to disclosure, and the professional believes disclosure is needed to prevent harm to the victim or others. (45 C.F.R. § 164.512(c)). A professional may disclose on behalf of a victim who is incapable of authorizing disclosure, if a government official states that the protected health information is not intended to be used against the victim, and that the information is immediately necessary for an ongoing investigation (45 C.F.R. § 164.512(c)(1)(B)). The victim should be informed, unless doing so would endanger the victim (45 C.F.R. § 164.512(c)(2)).

W. *TARASOFF* DUTY TO WARN

The California Supreme Court's decision in *Tarasoff v. Regents of the University of California,* 17 Cal. 3d 425 (1976), discussed in Chapter 6, imposes a duty on psychotherapists to warn potential victims of dangerous clients. The *Tarasoff* duty overrides confidentiality and privilege.

X. PROFESSIONAL CONSULTATION

By long tradition, professionals consult about cases, and, in so doing, discuss confidential information. (*See* APA *Code of Ethics*, Standard 405(b)). When the consultant is not the therapist's immediate supervisor, it is generally not necessary to reveal the client's identity. The APA *Code of Ethics* states, "When consulting with colleagues, (1) psychologists do not disclose confidential information that reasonably could lead to the identification of a client/patient . . . with whom they have a confidential relationship unless they have obtained the prior consent of the person . . . or the disclosure cannot be avoided, and . . . (2) they disclose information only to the extent necessary to achieve the purpose of the consultation."

Y. EMERGENCIES

In emergencies, it is sometimes essential to reveal confidential information. The HIPAA Privacy Rule authorizes emergency disclosure that serves the client's interests. (HIPAA, 45 C.F.R. §§ 164.510(b)(3); 164.512(j)). The NASW *Code of Ethics* provides, "The general expectation that social workers will keep information confidential does not apply when disclosure is necessary to prevent serious, foreseeable, and imminent harm to a client or other identifiable person."

Z. SUBPOENAS

There are two types of subpoena. First, a subpoena to testify at a trial, deposition, or other legal proceeding. A subpoena for testimony is often called a subpoena ad testificandum. Second, a subpoena for production of documents, often called a subpoena duces tecum. As mentioned above, a subpoena overrides ethical duties of confidentiality, but does not override privilege. A subpoena seeking privileged information can be quashed.

AA. LAW ENFORCEMENT REQUESTS

Laws allow law enforcement agencies to obtain access to certain confidential information. (*See* HIPAA, 45 C.F.R. 164.512(f)(3)).

BB. VOLUNTARY DISCLOSURE

When a patient willingly discloses to outsiders some or all of a privileged communication, any privilege is generally waived. (*See In re Clergy Cases*, 188 Cal. App. 4th 1224, 116 Cal. Rptr. 3d 360 (2010)).

CC. MENTAL HEALTH AND MEDICAL PROFESSIONALS TESTIFYING IN COURT SHOULD CONSULT AN ATTORNEY BEFORE TAKING CLIENT RECORDS TO COURT

When a professional takes confidential or privileged records to court, and uses the record to refresh memory while testifying, the opposing attorney has a right to read the record and ask about it. (Federal Rule of Evidence 612).

If the professional does not take records to court, but reads them in preparation for court, the opposing attorney may ask, "Did you review the client's clinical record before coming to court today?" If the answer is, "Yes," the attorney may ask the judge to require the professional to obtain the records so the lawyer can cross-examine about the records. The judge has discretion to require production of the record.

Mental health professionals are advised to consult an attorney about reviewing confidential and privileged records in preparation for testimony, and about taking records to court.

CHAPTER 3

EXPERT TESTIMONY

Expert testimony from mental health and medical professionals plays a vitally important role in litigation regarding mental illness and intellectual disability. This chapter outlines the rules of evidence governing expert testimony.

A. LAY OPINION TESTIMONY— FED. R. EVID. 701

Witnesses fall into two categories: Experts and lay witnesses. Experts normally testify in the form of opinion. Occasionally, one hears the statement, "Lay witnesses may not testify in the form of opinion." This is incorrect. In fact, lay witnesses offer opinions all the time. The point with lay witnesses is that they should, as much as possible, confine their testimony to specific factual information that is within their personal knowledge. The more specific, factual, and detailed a lay witness's testimony, the better. If some of a lay witness's testimony takes the form of opinion, that is okay.

Federal Rule of Evidence 701 sets the parameters on opinion testimony from lay witnesses. The Rule provides:

> If a witness is not testifying as an expert, testimony in the form of an opinion is limited to one that is: (a) rationally based on the witness's perception; (b) helpful to clearly understanding the witness's testimony or to determining a fact in issue; and (c) not based on scientific,

technical, or other specialized knowledge within the scope of Rule 702.

Courts approve lay opinion testimony on a broad range of subjects. Thus, a lay witness may opine on whether a person appeared ill, in pain, injured, drunk, or sober. A few examples of lay opinion testimony shed light on the array of situations where such testimony is allowed.

The Florida Court of Appeal's decision in *Bush v. State,* 809 So.2d 107 (Fla. Ct. App. 2002), involved very serious Munchausen Syndrome by Proxy, inflicted by a child's mother. When the child was finally rescued from her mother's "care," the child's health improved dramatically. It was not error for the prosecutor to offer lay testimony describing the child's improved health following rescue. The Court of Appeal noted, "A lay witness may describe a person's physical appearance using opinions that do not require special skill, so long as the opinions are based upon observations of the witness. . . . Here, the lay witness did not testify that Jennifer seemed 'healthier,' which would have been improper because [the lay witness] did not know Jennifer during her care with [the mother.]." (809 So. 2d at 119–120). If the lay witness had known Jennifer before and after her rescue, the witness could have testified that Jennifer appeared healthier.

In *Hicks v. State*, 6 So. 3d 1099 (Miss. Ct. App. 2009), the defendant had an argument with his seventy-two-year-old mother, so he took an ironing board and hit her with it multiple times. The defendant claimed he acted in self-defense when his mother came at him with a knife. An experienced police officer investigated the case and took photos. The officer testified as a lay witness about the minor nature of wounds on defendant. The defense objected that expert testimony was needed to describe injuries. The Mississippi Court of Appeal ruled that even if the officer's testimony crossed the line into expert testimony, any error was harmless. In all likelihood, it was not error for the officer to describe the defendant's injuries.

In *United States v. Yazzie*, 876 F.2d 1252 (9th Cir. 1992), the defendant was charged with statutory rape. The defense was reasonable mistake of age, that is, the defendant thought the victim was old enough to consent to sex. The defendant wanted to offer testimony from lay witnesses that the victim appeared to be at least sixteen. The trial judge rejected the lay testimony, but this was reversible error.

A lay witness may describe a person's state of mind: happy, sad, depressed, frightened, etc. In *People v. Acosta*, 338 P.3d 472 (Colo. Ct. App. 2014), defendant was caught in the act of inappropriate conduct with a child. The child's father angrily confronted the defendant. It was proper for the father to testify that defendant was "very guilty-looking."

May a lay witness offer an opinion that someone was insane or out of touch with reality? Clearly, a lay witness could describe a person's behavior, and testify to things the person did and said, from which an inference of mental illness might flow. In *People v. Clark*, 172 Mich. App. 1, 432 N.W.2d 173 (1988), defendant walked into a church, drew a gun, and robbed parishioners. At his robbery trial, it was proper for the parishioners to describe the defendant's behavior during the robbery. The Michigan Court of Appeals wrote, "The testimony of lay witnesses may be competent evidence on a defendant's mental illness." (432 N.W.2d at 178).

But may a lay witness go the next step and opine that someone was crazy? The general rule is yes, provided the lay witness has known the person a substantial time. Thus, in *Ex parte Milteer*, 571 So. 2d 998 (Ala. 1990), the Alabama Supreme Court wrote, "Generally, the testimony of a lay witness on the issue of sanity is competent and admissible where the lay witness has known the defendant for a long period of time." (p. 1000). In *Milteer*, the prosecutor offered lay testimony from two people who had brief contact with defendant. Over defense objection, the witnesses opined that defendant appeared sane. Allowing these opinions was reversible error because the witnesses did not know defendant well enough to form such an opinion.

Testimony from lay witnesses may support or contradict the observations of experts. (*People v. Corona*, 80 Cal. App. 3d 684, 708, 145 Cal. Rptr. 894, 907 (1978)).

There are limits on lay opinion testimony. Obviously, a lay witness must not offer expert testimony. In *State v. Duran*, 343 P.3d 207 (N.M. Ct. App. 2014), for example, the trial judge committed reversible error in allowing a forensic interviewer who testified as a lay witness to opine, "A majority of children she interviewed delayed in disclosing sexual abuse." (343 P.3d at 208). Testimony on how children disclose abuse, and, in particular, delayed disclosure, is the bailiwick of experts, not lay witnesses. In a child sexual abuse case from the military, the U.S. Court of Appeals for the Armed Forces ruled that a defendant's commanding officer should not have been allowed to testify that defendant's conduct was "indecent" or brought "discredit upon the Air Force." (*United States v. Littlewood*, 53 M.J. 349 (C.A.A.F. 2000)).

B. WHO MAY PROVIDE EXPERT TESTIMONY—FED. R. EVID. 702

In litigation involving mental illness and intellectual disability, expert testimony is provided by psychiatrists, psychologists, clinical social workers, and other clinicians. Rule 702 of the Federal Rules of Evidence describes who qualifies to provide expert testimony. The Rule states:

A witness who is qualified as an expert by knowledge, skill, experience, training, or education may testify in the form of an opinion or otherwise if: (a) the expert's scientific, technical, or other specialized knowledge will help the trier of fact to understand the evidence or to determine a fact in issue; (b) the testimony is based on sufficient facts or data; (c) the testimony is the product of reliable principles and methods; and (d) the expert has reliably applied the principles and methods to the facts of the case.

To qualify as an expert, a professional must possess sufficient "knowledge, skill, experience, training, or education." Unless a professional is clearly unqualified, deficiencies in qualifications go to the weight accorded the expert's testimony rather than admissibility. A professional need not be the foremost authority on a subject to provide expert testimony. Nor must a professional understand every nuance of a subject.

Before a professional may testify as an expert, the court must be satisfied that the professional is qualified. The normal procedure is for the proponent of the professional's testimony to put the professional on the stand, and ask questions about the person's education, training, and experience. The opposing attorney has the right to voir dire the witness in an effort to persuade the judge the person is not an expert. In most cases, there is no challenge to the expert's qualifications.

C.   FACTS ON WHICH EXPERT MAY BASE OPINION

Expert witnesses base their opinions on a broad range of facts and data. In the mental health arena, experts rely on many sources of information, including interviews of the individual, discussions with others, consultation with other experts, psychological tests, and written documentation, including hospital records and police reports. The rules of evidence permit experts to formulate court testimony based on the types of facts and data experts rely on in their normal, day-to-day work outside the courtroom. Federal Rule of Evidence 703 provides:

> An expert may base an opinion on facts or data in the case that the expert has been made aware of or personally observed. If experts in the particular field would reasonably rely on those kinds of facts or data in forming an opinion on the subject, they need not be admissible for the opinion to be admitted. But if the facts or data would otherwise be inadmissible, the proponent of the opinion may disclose them to the jury only if their probative value in helping the jury evaluate the opinion substantially outweighs their prejudicial effect.

Rule 703 specifies that experts may base opinions on information that is not admissible in evidence, so long as other experts in that field rely on such information. In the mental health field, experts routinely rely on hearsay that might or might not be admissible in court. Written hearsay includes clinical records, test results, and documents prepared by police and social services agencies. Verbal hearsay includes the patient's "history." A mental health professional acts properly when the professional bases expert testimony on such hearsay.

Although an expert's opinion may be based on inadmissible evidence, including inadmissible hearsay, Rule 703 provides, "But if the facts or data would otherwise be inadmissible, the proponent of the opinion may disclose them to the jury only if their probative value in helping the jury evaluate the opinion substantially outweighs their prejudicial effect." If there is no jury, and the judge is the trier of fact, the judge listens to the hearsay and determines how much, if any, weight to give it. When there is a jury, the judge balances the probative value of the inadmissible hearsay against the probability the jury will place too much weight on the hearsay.

Courts agree that it is improper to use an expert as a mere conduit to get inadmissible hearsay before a jury. (*I–CA Enterprises v. Palram Americas, Inc.*, 185 Cal. Rptr. 3d 24, 235 Cal. App. 4th 257, 286 (2015)).

D. TESTIMONY ON ULTIMATE ISSUES

In every case, there are ultimate facts and ultimate legal issues. The ultimate facts are the facts a party must prove to prevail in litigation. Suppose, for example, that Sue broke into a house in order to steal. Sue is charged with burglary, which was defined at common law as the breaking and entering of the dwelling house of another at night with the intent to commit a felony therein. The ultimate facts are: (1) breaking, (2) entering, (3) the dwelling house of another, (4) at night, and (5) Sue intended to commit a felony inside the dwelling.

In a rape prosecution, the crime is defined as sexual intercourse accomplished by force and against the will of the victim. Penetration is an ultimate fact.

In the burglary case, lay witnesses could testify to the ultimate facts required for conviction. In the rape case, the victim or an expert witness could testify regarding penetration.

The ultimate legal issue in the burglary and rape cases is whether the defendant is guilty or innocent. Witnesses may testify to ultimate facts, but not ultimate legal issues such as guilt or innocence.

In civil commitment proceedings, whether a person is mentally ill and in an ultimate fact. In *In re B.O.T.*, 378 Mont. 198, 203, 342 P.3d 981 (2015), the Montana Supreme Court wrote, "The professional person may testify as to the ultimate issue of whether the respondent is suffering from a mental disorder and requires commitment. . . ."

Federal Rule of Evidence 704 deals with ultimate issue testimony:

(a) An opinion is not objectionable just because it embraces an ultimate issue.

(b) In a criminal case, an expert must not state an opinion about whether the defendant did or did not have a mental state or condition that constitutes an element of the crime charged or of a defense. Those matters are for the trier of fact alone.

Rule 704(b) has a direct bearing on expert testimony from mental health professionals. The Rule prohibits an expert from offering an opinion that a defendant did or did not have the mens rea required for a crime. Nor may an expert testify that a defendant met the requirements of the insanity defense. The Advisory Committee Note to Rule 704(b) explains:

The purpose of [Rule 704(b)] is to eliminate the confusing spectacle of competing expert witnesses testifying to directly contradictory conclusions as to the ultimate legal issue to be found by the trier of fact [*e.g.*, insanity]. Under [Rule 704(b)], expert psychiatric testimony would be limited to presenting and explaining their diagnoses, such as whether a defendant had a severe mental disease or defect and what the characteristics of such a disease or defect, if any, many have been. The basis for this limitation on expert testimony in insanity cases is ably stated by the American Psychiatric Association:

"It is clear that psychiatrists are experts in medicine, not the law. As such, it is clear that the psychiatrist's first obligation and expertise in the courtroom is to 'do psychiatry,' *i.e.*, to present medical information and opinion about the defendant's mental state and motivation and to explain in detail the reason for his medical-psychiatric conclusions. When, however, 'ultimate issue' questions are formulated by the law and put to the expert witness who must then say 'yea' or 'nay,' then the expert witness is required to make a leap in logic. He no longer addresses himself to medical concepts but instead must infer or intuit what is in fact unspeakable, namely, the probable relationship between medical concepts and legal or moral constructs such as free will. These impermissible leaps in logic made by expert witnesses confuse the jury. Juries thus find themselves listening to conclusory and seemingly contradictory psychiatric testimony that defendants are either 'sane' or 'insane' or that they do or do not meet the relevant legal test for insanity. This state of affairs does considerable injustice to psychiatry and, we believe, possibly criminal defendants. In fact, in many criminal trials both prosecution and defense psychiatrists do agree about the nature and even the extent of mental disorder exhibited by the defendant at the time of the act."

Psychiatrists, of course, must be permitted to testify fully about the defendant's diagnosis, mental state and motivation (in clinical and commonsense terms) at the time of the alleged act so as to permit the jury or judge to reach the ultimate conclusion about which they and only they are expert. Determining whether a criminal defendant was legally insane is a matter for legal fact-finders, not for experts.

Moreover, the rationale for precluding ultimate opinion psychiatric testimony extends beyond the insanity defense to any ultimate mental state of the defendant that is relevant to the legal conclusion sought to be proven. The committee has fashioned its rule 704 provision to reach all such "ultimate" issues, *e.g.,* premeditation in a homicide case, or lack of predisposition in entrapment.

Christopher Mueller and Laird Kirkpatrick explain how Rule 704(b) is designed to work in practice: "Under FRE 704(b) a psychiatrist or other expert should not couch her testimony in terms of the legal elements in the insanity defense. Instead she should stay one step back, explaining the basis for her diagnosis, describing the defendant's condition by giving the diagnosis itself and the characteristics of the affliction, and saying how such a condition would or might affect the ability of an ordinary person to appreciate the nature and quality or wrongfulness of his acts or conform his conduct to the law, although these last points get so close to the ultimate issue that courts sometimes balk. What FRE 704(b) aims to prevent is expert testimony that goes directly to the legal conclusion. An expert should not testify, for example, that the defendant could not appreciate the wrongfulness of his acts or conform his conduct to the requirements of law." (Christopher B. Mueller & Laird C. Kirkpatrick, *Evidence,* § 7.13, pp. 678–679 (5th ed. 2012)).

Despite Rule 704(b), the Advisory Committee Note, the American Psychiatric Association, and professors Mueller and Kirkpatrick, experts in insanity cases routinely violate the spirit and letter of Rule 704(b) by opining on what was going through a defendant's mind at the time of a crime, and whether the defendant knew the nature and quality of the act, or whether it was wrong. Unless the judge prohibits such testimony, it is up to the cross-examining attorney to critique the expert's testimony.

In *Edwards v. State*, 464 S.W.3d 473 (Ark. Ct. App. 2015), the Arkansas Court of Appeals placed proper limits on expert testimony. The defendant was a regular customer at a bar until he was banned for threatening to kill a bartender and everyone in the bar. When defendant returned to the bar, he was asked to leave. He left, but returned with a shotgun and killed one person and tried to kill another. At his murder trial, defendant offered expert testimony that defendant's mental illness prevented him from forming the specific intent to kill. The Court of Appeals rejected expert testimony that a defendant had or did not have the ability to form the intent to commit murder. The court wrote, "The decision whether Edwards had the requisite intent to commit his crime was an ultimate issue for the jury to decide, and it was not proper for any witness—even an expert—to testify concerning that issue."

E. REASONABLE CERTAINTY

When eliciting an expert's opinion, it is common for an attorney to ask, "Doctor, do you have an opinion, based on a reasonable degree of certainty, whether Ms. Jones was mentally ill?" (*See State v. Kucharski*, 866 N.W.2d 658 (Wis. 2015)). In *People v. Gilmore*, 210 Ill. Dec. 471, 473, 653 N.E.2d 58, 60, 273 Ill. App. 3d 996 (1995), for example, an expert testified, "to a reasonable degree of medical and psychiatric certainty defendant was mentally ill and legally insane at the time of the alleged offense." *Gilmore* illustrates the so-called "reasonable certainty" standard: An expert must be reasonable certain the opinion is correct.

The rules of evidence do not mandate experts to frame testimony in terms of reasonable certainty. Yet, attorneys so often ask questions in terms of reasonable certainty that it is helpful to understand the meaning of the phrase. The answer is, no one knows the meaning of reasonable certainty. Jeff Lewin explored the development of "reasonable certainty," and concluded: "Although judges expect, and sometimes insist, that expert opinions be expressed with 'reasonable medical certainty,' and although attorneys ritualistically intone the phrase, no one knows what it means!" (Jeff L. Lewin, The Genesis and Evolution of Legal Uncertainty About "Reasonable Medical Certainty," 57 *Maryland Law Review* 380 (1998)).

Expert witnesses do not have to be completely certain their opinion is correct. The Iowa Supreme Court observed in *State v. Tyler*, 867 N.W.2d 136 (Iowa 2015), "There is no requirement that the expert be able to express an opinion with absolute certainty. A lack of absolute certainty goes to the weight of the expert's testimony, not its admissibility." At the same time, experts cannot speculate or guess. The California Court of Appeal wrote in *Pedeferri v. Seidner Enterprises*, 216 Cal. App. 4th 359, 375, 163 Cal. Rptr. 3d 55 (2013), "Where an expert bases his conclusion upon assumptions which are not supported by the record, . . . his conclusion has no evidentiary value and should be excluded." Thus, experts may not guess, but, at the same time, they do not have to be 100% certain they are right. Reasonable certainty lies somewhere between guesswork and certainty—closer to the latter.

Not only does reasonable certainty have no clear meaning, the phrase can cause confusion because it is a legal term, not a term employed in medicine or mental health. Glenn Bradford comments, "Many lawyers and judges believe the phrase is a medical term of art. Physician commentators, however, have described the phrase as a legal term of art." (Glenn F. Bradford, Dissecting Missouri's Requirement of "Reasonable Medical Certainty," 57 *Missouri Bar Journal* 136, 137 (2001)).

Norman Poythress writes, "I've always had a pretty healthy skepticism about phrases like 'reasonable medical certainty.' . . . Left undefined, there is a risk that lay jurors will think that the opinions are somehow an outgrowth of quasi-objective, scientific investigation. . . ." (Norman G. Poythress, Concerning Reform in Expert Testimony: an Open Letter from a Practicing Psychologist, 6 *Law and Human Behavior* 39–43, 41 (1982)).

Gary Melton and his colleagues observe, "There is a danger that, because of the law's preference for certainty, experts will over-reify their observations and reach beyond legitimate interpretations of the data. . . ." (Gary B. Melton, John Petrila, Norman G. Poythress & Christopher Slobogin, *Psychological Evaluations for the Courts: A Handbook for Mental Health Professionals and Lawyers,* p. 11 (2nd ed. 1997)).

In the final analysis, it would probably be better to jettison reasonable certainty. Some appellate courts have. (*See State v. DeLeon,* 319 P.3d 463 (Hawai'i 2014)). For now, however, attorneys continue asking,

"Do you have an opinion, based on a reasonable degree of certainty, whether _____?"

The concept of reasonable certainty should not be confused with the burden of proof. The burden of proof is the level of certainty by which a jury must be persuaded by the evidence presented by the party with the burden of proof. Three burdens of proof are used: (a) Beyond a reasonable doubt, (b) Preponderance of the evidence, and (c) Clear and convincing evidence.

Beyond a reasonable doubt is used in criminal cases, and is the most difficult burden to meet. A prosecutor must prove the defendant guilty beyond a reasonable doubt. Most civil litigation uses the less demanding preponderance of the evidence standard. Under the preponderance standard, the party with the burden of proof need only convince the jury that it is more likely than not that the party should win. The third burden of proof, clear and convincing evidence, is reserved for a small number of civil cases where the stakes are particularly high, including termination of parental rights and involuntary psychiatric hospitalization.

Burdens of proof are legal concepts that are not reducible to simple percentages. Yet, a measure of insight is afforded by comparing beyond a reasonable doubt to 95% certainty, preponderance of evidence to 51% certainty, and clear and convincing evidence to 75% certainty.

As discussed above, in many courts, experts must be reasonably certain their opinions are right. It is important to understand that the certainty needed for expert testimony does *not* vary with the type of litigation. Experts do not have to be more certain in criminal cases, where the burden of proof is highest, than in civil cases. Regardless of the type of litigation—criminal or civil—experts should ensure the correctness of opinions.

Occasionally, attorneys ask experts whether they are certain of their opinion beyond a reasonable doubt or by a preponderance of the evidence. An accurate response to such a question is, "Counsel, when I reach an opinion, I do not employ the legal concept of burden of proof. Burdens of proof are legal constructs, and are not used in psychology. Instead, I use clinical and scientific principles to reach my opinion. In reaching my opinion, I took all the steps I could to ensure that my opinion is correct. I am reasonably certain of my opinion, and, by reasonably certain, I mean I am confident my opinion is correct."

F. NOVEL SCIENTIFIC EVIDENCE: *FRYE* AND *DAUBERT*

When expert testimony is based on scientific or technical principles—especially principles that are unproven or novel—the attorney opposing the expert may ask the judge to hold a hearing to determine whether the science or technology underlying proposed expert testimony is valid and reliable. Such hearings are called *Frye* or *Daubert* hearings, after two famous cases, *Frye v. United States,* 54 App. D.C. 46, 293 F. 1013 (1923) and *Daubert v. Merrell Dow Pharmaceuticals, Inc.,* 509 U.S. 579 (1993).

Frye was decided in 1923 by the Court of Appeals for the District of Columbia, and dealt with an early version of the polygraph. The court fashioned a test to evaluate the reliability of scientific principles underlying expert testimony. The court ruled that expert testimony based on novel scientific principles cannot be admitted in evidence until the principles are generally accepted as reliable by the scientific community, that is, until the principles pass the admittedly fuzzy line that separates novelty from general acceptance. This test for scientific evidence is called the general acceptance test or, simply, *Frye*.

During a *Frye* hearing, expert testimony is offered concerning the validity and reliability (*i.e.*, general acceptance) of the disputed scientific principle. If the judge finds general acceptance, the expert testimony is allowed. However, if the judge finds that the principle underlying the expert testimony is not generally accepted as reliable, the judge excludes the testimony.

For most of the twentieth century, *Frye* was the dominant test to evaluate novel scientific evidence. Over the years, *Frye* was criticized. The basic criticism was that *Frye*'s requirement of general acceptance excludes expert testimony based on science or technology that has not achieved general acceptance, but is nevertheless sufficiently reliable for use in court. Criticism of *Frye* culminated in the U.S. Supreme Court's 1993 decision in *Daubert v. Merrell Dow Pharmaceuticals, Inc.*, where the Court rejected *Frye* and replaced it with a broadened test for scientific evidence.

As is true with *Frye,* under *Daubert,* an attorney objects that expert testimony is based on unreliable scientific principles or techniques, and requests a hearing—called a *Daubert* hearing. Unlike *Frye,* where the only issue was general acceptance, a judge conducting a *Daubert* hearing considers *all* evidence shedding light on reliability. The judge considers whether the scientific principle underlying the proposed expert testimony has been subjected to testing by the scientific method. Has the principle been scrutinized by peer review and publication? Is there an established error rate when the principle or technique is used? Are there standards governing use of the principle? Finally, borrowing from *Frye,* is the principle generally accepted as reliable in the scientific community? A scientific principle or technique that has yet to achieve general acceptance may nevertheless be sufficiently reliable under *Daubert* to gain admission in court.

The *Daubert* decision concerned expert testimony based on science. Following *Daubert,* there was uncertainty whether *Daubert* applied to expert testimony that combines science and professional judgment and interpretation. Thus, does *Daubert* apply to much of the expert testimony provided by physicians and mental health professionals? In 1999, the Supreme Court answered in the affirmative in *Kumho Tire Company, Ltd. v. Carmichael*, 526 U.S. 137, 119 S. Ct. 137 (1999). The Supreme Court ruled, "*Daubert*'s general holding—setting forth the trial judge's gatekeeping obligation—applies not only to testimony based on scientific knowledge, but also to testimony based on technical and other specialized knowledge." (526 U.S. at 141).

The Supreme Court's rulings in *Daubert* and *Kumho* are only binding on federal courts, and do not compel states to abandon *Frye*. Most states have jettisoned *Frye* in favor of *Daubert*. States retaining *Frye* include California, Illinois, New Mexico, and Washington. (*See In Matter of Detention of Pettis,* 352 P.3d 841 (Wash. Ct. App. 2015) (*Frye* hearing on instrument intended to assess risk of reoffending among sex offenders)).

In the vast majority of cases involving expert testimony, there is no *Frye* or *Daubert* hearing. The expert gets on the witness stand, is qualified, testifies, is cross-examined, and that is the end of it. *Frye* or *Daubert* only arise in exceptional cases.

A few states (*e.g.*, Arizona, California) have a rule that *Frye/Daubert* does not apply to expert testimony in the form of opinion. (*See Wilson v. Phillips*, 73 Cal. App. 4th 250, 86 Cal. Rptr. 2d 204 (1999)). In *Logerquist v. McVey*, 196 Ariz. 470, 1 P.3d 113 (2000), for example, the Arizona Supreme Court wrote, "To put it simply, *Frye* is inapplicable when a qualified witness offers relevant testimony or conclusions based on experience and observation about human behavior for the purpose of explaining that behavior." (1 P.3d at 123).

The premise supporting this rule is that jurors are not likely to be misled or over-impressed by opinion testimony. Jurors, so the theory goes, can evaluate the worth of opinion, especially with the aid of cross-examination. By contrast, jurors may be awestruck or blindsided by machines, devices, and techniques that profess to be based on science, and that purport to yield definitive answers to complex questions. Jurors and cross-examining lawyers are not well equipped to peer into "little black scientific boxes" to determine whether they yield reliable data. Out of concern that jurors will be too impressed by little black boxes, courts limit *Frye/Daubert* to expert testimony based on novel scientific principles, machines, devices, and techniques.

The problem with the approach employed in Arizona and California is that opinion testimony can be just as misleading, inaccurate, obtuse, invalid, and unreliable—just as likely to blindside a jury—as anything emerging from the scientific version of a little black box. Moreover, there is little reason to believe cross-examining attorneys are better at dissecting opinion testimony than testimony based on devices or techniques. If the primary concern is protecting juries from "junk science," the best approach is to apply *Frye/Daubert* to any expert testimony of dubious validity or reliability, whether in the form of opinion or a little black box.

CHAPTER 4
CRIMINAL LAW

Chapter 4 discusses the role of mental illness and mental health professionals in criminal law. Not a day goes by that police, prosecutors, defense attorneys, probation and parole officers, jail and prison authorities, and judges do not interact with individuals suffering mental illness, addiction, and intellectual disability. It is a sad commentary that America's jails and prisons are home to hundreds of thousands of mentally ill inmates. Indeed, there are more mentally ill people in jail than in the hospital.

Most readers of this book have completed the course on criminal law. Nevertheless, to set the stage for the role of mental illness in criminal law, it is useful to review a few basic principles of criminal law. Crimes have a physical component and a mental component. The physical component is the actus reus. The mental component is the mens rea, or criminal intent. The U.S. Supreme Court put it colorfully when it wrote that crime requires an "evil-meaning mind and an evil-doing hand." (*Dixon v. United States*, 548 U.S. 1, 5, 126 S. Ct. 2437 (2006)).

All crimes have an actus reus. Most, but not all, crimes have a mens rea. Strict liability offenses have no mens rea.

A. ACTUS REUS

The actus reus of crime requires a voluntary muscular movement. The person must deliberately move the body. If a person's body moves while the person is unconscious, this is not an act for criminal law purposes. For example, a person whose body moves in the midst of a grand mal seizure does not commit an act. Unconsciousness is a defense against criminal charges.

Normally, the actus reus is an affirmative act—pulling a trigger, taking someone's car. In rare cases, a person commits a crime by doing *nothing,* failing to act. This is so, for example, when a person who has a duty to assist another fails to provide assistance. A duty to act—and thus liability for failing to act—can arise when: (1) A statute imposes a duty to act; (2) There is a contractual relationship that imposes a duty to act; (3) A relationship such as parent and child imposes a duty to act; (4) An individual voluntarily assumes the care or protection of another; and (5) An individual creates a risk that threatens another.

B. MENS REA

Within criminal law, few subjects are more complex than criminal intent—mens rea. Mens rea terms include malice, willful, intentional, knowing, reckless, and negligent. Sometimes the same word, *e.g.,* malice, is found in different crimes, and has a different meaning in each crime. Thus, arson was defined at common law as "the malicious burning of the dwelling house of another." Murder is the "unlawful killing of a human being with malice aforethought." The meaning of malice is not the same in arson and murder.

The Model Penal Code (MPC) has four mens rea states: purposely, knowingly, recklessly, and negligently (MPC § 2.02(2)). A person acts "purposely" when it is the person's conscious object to bring about a specific result. Thus, Sue acts purposely when she shoots Beth, intending to kill Beth. A person acts "knowingly" when the person is aware that her conduct is practically certain to cause a particular result. Juan acts knowingly when he transports a truck load of heroine, realizing what he is transporting. A person acts "recklessly" when the person is subjectively aware that her conduct creates a substantial risk of harm, and the person consciously disregards the risk. Francis is reckless when she knows she is driving in a school zone where the speed is 25 miles an hour, and that children are playing nearby, but Francis intentionally disregards the risk she creates by driving through the school zone at 100 miles an hour. A person acts negligently when she is not aware of the risk she creates, but a reasonable person would be aware.

Criminal intent is often challenging to prove. Intent is invisible. It is a state of mind. If the defendant made inculpatory statements before trial, those statements are admissible against the defendant under the hearsay doctrine called party admissions, so long as the corpus delecti is established. In addition to the defendant's words, prosecutors prove mens rea with eyewitness testimony, DNA, fingerprints, and circumstantial evidence. Often, intent is established with evidence of how the crime was committed.

The common law distinguished between specific intent and general intent crimes. Many states still recognize the distinction. The MPC, and some states, abandoned the specific/general intent dichotomy.

GENERAL INTENT

All that is required for a general intent crime is to intentionally do the actus reus. With a general intent crime, there is no requirement that the defendant intend to accomplish anything in addition to the actus reus. Nor is there a requirement that the defendant commit the actus reus with a special motive or desire. As the California Supreme Court explained, "When the definition of a crime consists of only the description of a particular act, without reference to intent to do a further act or achieve a future consequence, we ask whether the defendant intended to do the proscribed act. This is deemed to be a general criminal intent." (*People v. Hood*, 1 Cal. 3d 444, 456–457, 462 P.2d 370 (1969)).

Battery is a general intent offense. Battery is willful use of force upon another. The defendant must willfully (*i.e.*, intentionally) use force on another. It is not necessary that the defendant know the conduct is against the law. Nor is it necessary that the defendant use force for any particular purpose, or with any particular motive. All that is required is that the defendant intend to use force upon another.

SPECIFIC INTENT

Specific intent crimes fall into two categories: First, the definition of the crime provides that the defendant must have a goal of achieving something *in addition* to the actus reus. The California Supreme

Court explained in *Hood*, "When the definition [of a crime] refers to the defendant's intent to do some further act or achieve some additional consequence, the crime is deemed to be one of specific intent." (1 Cal. 3d at 457).

With the second category of specific intent crimes, the definition of the crime provides that the defendant must commit the actus reus with a particular motive or desire. The two categories of specific intent often overlap.

Theft is a specific intent crime. At common law, theft was the trespassory caption and asportation of the personal property of another with the intent to steal. The accused must perform the actus reus (tresspassorily take and carry away the personal property of another), and, *in addition*, must intend to steal the property. Burglary is another specific intent offense. At common law, burglary was the breaking and entering of the dwelling house of another at night with the intent to commit a felony therein. The defendant must break and enter and, *in addition*, must intend to commit a felony inside.

Mental illness can play a role in determining whether a person had the mens rea for a crime. (*See State v. Graham*, 113 A.3d 1102 (Maine 2015)). In this regard, it is important to determine whether the crime is general or specific intent. More is said on this point later.

C. DEFENSES

A defense is a set of facts or circumstances that may prevent conviction for an offense, or lower the seriousness of the crime. Defenses can be divided into three categories: (1) Failure of proof defenses; (2) Affirmative defenses; and (3) Public policy defenses.

FAILURE OF PROOF DEFENSES

The prosecutor must prove every element of the charged crime beyond a reasonable doubt. As well, the prosecutor must prove defendant was the perpetrator. One way to defend a case is to attack the prosecution's evidence in the hope of raising a reasonable doubt that the prosecution met its burden of proof. As explained by the California Court of Appeal, "When a defense is one that negates proof of an element of the charged offense, the defendant need only raise a reasonable doubt of the existence of that fact. This is so because the defense goes directly to guilt or innocence." (*People v. Gonzales*, 74 Cal. App. 4th 382, 88 Cal. Rptr. 2d 111 (1999)). Lawyers and judges often use the term "failure of proof defense" to describe defenses that seek to raise a reasonable doubt that the prosecution proved one or more elements of the crime, or the defendant's identity.

Alibi is a failure of proof defense. If the defendant was in Paris, France when the bank was robbed in New York City, the prosecution failed to prove identity. Mistake of fact is another failure of proof defense. If the defendant is charged with stealing wooden beams from a construction site, but the defendant convinces the jury that he thought beams were abandoned, and he could take them, then the prosecution failed to prove intent to steal. Accident is another failure of proof defense. If the defendant is charged with involuntary manslaughter for causing a traffic accident, but the jury is convinced the crash was an accident, and nobody's fault, then the prosecution failed to prove that defendant had criminal intent. Sometimes, mental illness provides a failure of proof defense. For example, a person who is psychotic might not take property intending to steal it.

AFFIRMATIVE DEFENSES

An affirmative defense asserts facts that are *separate* from the elements of the charged crime, and that, if true, create a defense. In *People v. Nobel*, 100 Cal. App. 4th 184, 189, 121 Cal. Rptr. 2d 918 (2002), the California Court of Appeal explained, "An affirmative defense is one which does not negate an essential element of a cause of action or charged crime, and instead presents new matter to excuse or justify conduct that would otherwise lead to liability."

Self-defense is an affirmative defense. The elements of self-defense are separate from the elements of murder or assault. Other affirmative defenses include necessity, duress, and insanity. (*See* MPC § 4.03(1); "Mental disease or defect excluding responsibility is an affirmative defense.")

PUBLIC POLICY DEFENSES

In a few situations, the legislature decides individuals should not be prosecuted even though they may be guilty! The statute of limitations is one such defense, based on the public policy that it is unfair to prosecute individuals if so much time has elapsed since the crime that it will be difficult for the defendant to mount a defense. Evidence may be hard to find. Witnesses may have died, forgotten what happened, or moved away.

JUSTIFICATION OR EXCUSE

By long tradition, affirmative defenses are justifications or excuses. With a justification defense, defendant's conduct under the circumstances was morally correct. Self-defense is a justification defense. A person who kills in self-defense takes a life, but only because the person who died was attacking the defender. It is unfortunate a life was lost, but, under the circumstances, the defender did the morally correct thing. Society makes the value judgment that it can be justifiable to kill in self-defense.

An excuse differs from a justification as follows: With a justification such as self-defense, the defendant did the right thing under the circumstances. By contrast, with an excuse, defendant did the wrong thing; defendant's conduct was not morally defensible. Yet, despite the fact that what the defendant did was wrong, we afford a defense because there is something wrong with the defendant; some defect that renders the defendant morally blameless. The insanity defense is an excuse. When an insane person kills an innocent victim because the insane person thinks the victim is from Mars and is about to vaporize him with a ray gun, we do not say the insane person did the right thing. It was wrong. Yet, because the insane person's mental illness renders the person morally blameless; it is wrong to punish the person.

There was a time when the consequences for a defendant differed depending on whether a defense was a justification or an excuse. No more. Today, justifications and excuses are complete defenses. If the jury accepts the defense, the defendant is acquitted. As a practical matter, a defendant does not care whether a defense is an excuse or a justification, so long as it works! Today, courts often use the words justification and excuse interchangeably. Yet, because it is the tradition to distinguish excuse from justification, and because the moral baggage attached to each differs, it is useful to observe the distinction.

D. MENTAL ILLNESS AND CRIMINAL LAW

A person's mental condition can be relevant at all stages of the criminal justice process. Police officers encounter the mentally disturbed all the time, and decide whether to arrest the person for committing a crime (*e.g.*, urinating in public), take the person to a hospital, or leave the person alone.

American jails and prisons have medical and mental health professionals on staff. Needless to say, the quality of mental health care varies from institution to institution. Yet, thousands of inmates receive medication and counseling services.

When arrest occurs, prosecutors consider mental illness in deciding what, if any, charges to bring. Some cities have a mental health court. Other cities have drug court, veteran's court, or other specialized courts.

At sentencing, the defendant's mental status is a factor in deciding the proper disposition.

At the trial stage, a person's mental condition can be relevant for four purposes: (1) Defendant's mental condition *at the time of the offense* may meet the requirements of the insanity defense; (2) Defendant's mental condition *at the time of the offense* may suggest that the defendant lacked the mens rea for the crime; (3) Defendant's mental condition *at the time of trial* may render the defendant incompetent to stand trial; and (4) "[E]xecution of the intellectually disabled contravenes the Eighth Amendment's prohibition on cruel and unusual punishment." (*Atkins v. Virginia*, 536 U.S. 304, 122 S. Ct. 2242 (2002). *See also*, *Brumfield v. Cain,* 135 S. Ct. 2269 (2015) (defendant was convicted of murdering an off-duty police officer, and sentenced to death; defendant requested an opportunity to prove that he was intellectually disabled, and could not be executed; trial judge refused to provide an evidentiary hearing; this was error); *Ford v. Wainwright*, 477 U.S. 399, 106 S. Ct. 2595 (1986)).

E. INSANITY DEFENSE

The insanity defense is an excuse. The defendant's wrongful conduct is excused because of the defendant's mental illness or intellectual disability. Contrary to popular belief, the insanity defense is rarely deployed. Henry Fradella writes, "The insanity defense is used quite rarely. It is only raised in approximately 1% of all felony cases and, when invoked, the insanity defense is successful less than 25% of the time." (Henry F. Fradella, *From Insanity to Diminished Capacity: Mental Illness and Criminal Excuse in Contemporary American Law,* p. 15 (2007). (*See State v. Murphy*, 2015 WL 2189817 (Me. 2015) (psychiatric inpatient who attacked a staff member with a sharp pen, causing injury, did not carry his burden of proof to establish insanity defense)).

A high profile example of a failed attempt at the insanity defense involved the July 16, 2015 conviction by a Colorado jury of James Holmes for multiple counts of first degree murder in the Aurora, Colorado movie theater shooting. On July 20, 2012, Holmes killed twelve people and injured seventy others when he opened fire in a crowded theater with a shotgun, a semiautomatic rifle, and a pistol. Holmes had recently broken up with a girlfriend and flunked out of graduate school. He planned the crime meticulously. The defense asserted the insanity defense, but the jury did not buy it.

The law has long recognized the impropriety of punishing someone whose mental illness deprives the person of culpability. As early as the 1700s in England, a "mad man" who did not know what he was doing any "more than a brute or a wild beast" was immune from punishment.

The American Psychiatric Association (APA) notes: "The insanity defense has always been grounded in the belief that there are defendants whose mental conditions are so impaired at the time of the crime that it would be unfair to punish them for their acts." (APA, Position Statement on the Insanity Defense, 2014).

There are four variations of the insanity defense, each tracing its origins to the famous murder trial of Daniel M'Naghten in London in 1843. (8 Eng. Rep. 718 (1843)). M'Naghten gradually came to believe that the government was following and persecuting him. Armed with two pistols, M'Naghten went to the home of Prime Minister Robert Peel in London, intent on killing him. He followed a man he believed was Peel, pulled a pistol, and shot the man in the back. A police officer apprehended M'Naghten before he could shoot again. The victim was not the Prime Minister, but his private secretary, Edward Drummond, who succumbed to his wound. The jury acquitted M'Naghten, based on insanity. The acquittal caused an uproar that led to a revised test for legal insanity, the M'Naghten test.

The M'Naghten test provides: "To establish a defense on the ground of insanity it must be clearly proved that, at the time of committing the act, the party accused was laboring under such a defect of reason, from disease of the mind, as not to know the nature and quality of the act he was doing, or, if he did know it, that he did not know that what he was doing was wrong."

M'Naghten's "disease of the mind" refers to mental illness or intellectual disability. This is not to say that mental illness itself is a defense. Most seriously mentally ill defendants, including those with schizophrenia, do not meet M'Naghten.

Psychopathy is a personality disorder listed in the DSM–5, where it is called Antisocial Personality Disorder. (DSM–5, at p. 659). Psychopaths lack empathy for others, and do not feel guilt for wrongdoing. Psychopaths often engage in criminal activity and deceit. Could a psychopath use the disorder as the basis for an insanity plea? The answer is no. Courts and legislatures agree that psychopathy is not "insanity" for purposes of the insanity defense. The Model Penal Code agrees, providing, "The terms 'mental disease or defect' do not include an abnormality manifested only by repeated criminal or otherwise antisocial conduct." (MPC § 4.01(2)).

M'Naghten focuses on the defendant's cognitive ability to understand one of the following: (1) The nature and quality of her act, that is, what she was doing, or (2) If she understood what she was doing, that what she was doing was wrong. Suppose a psychotic individual strangles the governor, thinking the governor is a zombie trying to eat her brain. The defendant's psychosis deprived her of an understanding of what she did—she thought she was killing a zombie, not a human being. Alternatively, suppose the defendant knew she was strangling the governor, but she did it because auditory hallucinations told her the governor was about kill everyone in the state. In this scenario, defendant knew what she was doing, but she didn't know it was wrong.

The meaning of "wrong" in M'Naghten has caused confusion. Does "wrong" mean against the law? Does it mean morally wrong? Must the defendant be *subjectively* aware that her conduct is against the law and/or morally wrong? In *United States v. Ewing*, 494 F.3d 607, 621 (7th Cir. 2007), the court explained, "We conclude that wrongfulness for purposes of the federal insanity defense statute is defined by reference to objective societal or public standards of moral wrongness, not the defendant's subjective personal standards of moral wrongfulness." In *State v. Singleton*, 211 N.J. 157, 48 A.3d 285, 295–296 (2012), the New Jersey Supreme Court wrote, "A majority of states following the M'Naghten test have interpreted 'wrong' as encompassing legal as well as moral wrong."

Approximately half the states and the federal government retain M'Naghten. The federal insanity defense states: "It is an affirmative defense to a prosecution under any Federal statute that, at the time of the commission of the acts constituting the offense, the defendant, as a result of a severe mental disease or defect, was unable to appreciate the nature and quality or the wrongfulness of his acts. Mental disease or defect does not otherwise constitute a defense." (18 U.S.C. § 17(a)).

M'Naghten focuses entirely on the defendant's cognitive capacity to know what she is doing, or to distinguish right from wrong. M'Naghten disregards the impact mental illness can have on a person's ability to control their behavior—volitional control. A few states that use M'Naghten add to it the so-called "irresistible impulse test." This test allows a defendant who knew what she was doing, and who knew it was wrong, to argue that her mental illness deprived her of self-control. (*See Commonwealth v. DiPadova*, 460 Mass. 424, 951 N.E.2d 891 (2011)).

M'Naghten and irresistible impulse are difficult for defendants to satisfy. In most cases, mental illness, even serious mental illness, does not completely destroy a person's cognitive capacity to know what she is doing, or to understand that it is wrong. (*See People v. Blakely*, 230 Cal. App. 4th 771, 178 Cal. Rptr. 3d 876 (2014)). Yet, destruction of cognitive capacity is required by M'Naghten. Paul Robinson and his colleagues write that M'Naghten "requires absolute inability to tell that one's conduct is wrong." (Paul H. Robinson, Mathew G. Kussmaul, Camber M. Stoddard, Iiya Rudyak & Andreas Kuersten, The American Criminal Code: General Defenses, 7 *Journal of Legal Analysis* 37, at p. 78 (2015)). Similarly, with irresistible impulse, in most cases, mental illness does not completely eliminate volitional control.

More than a dozen states broaden M'Naghten/irresistible impulse by adopting the *Model Penal Code* (MPC) definition of insanity: "A person is not responsible for criminal conduct if at the time of such conduct, as a result of mental disease or defect, he lacks *substantial* capacity either to appreciate the criminality [wrongfulness] of his conduct or to conform his conduct to the requirements of the law." (MPC § 4.01(1)).

Use of the word "substantial" in MPC § 4.01(a) introduces shades of gray into the insanity defense. The Explanatory Note to § 4.01(a) states, "The standard does not require a total lack of capacity, only that capacity be insubstantial." (MPC § 4.01, Explanatory Note, p. 174). A delusional defendant who has *some* idea of what she is doing, or that it is wrong, is not insane under M'Naghten, but might lack *substantial* capacity under the MPC. Even under the MPC's more flexible test, however, few mentally ill defendants qualify for the insanity defense. (*See State v. Anderson*, 357 Wis. 2d 337, 851 N.W.2d 760 (2014)).

When a defendant is found not guilty by reason of insanity, the defendant does not walk out of court a free person. If the acquitted defendant poses a danger to self or others, the person is committed to an institution. (*See* Model Penal Code § 4.08).

Four states abolished the insanity defense: Idaho, Kansas, Montana, and Utah. (*See* Idaho Code § 18–207(1); Kan. Stat. Ann. § 22–3220; Mont. Code Ann. § 46–14–104; Utah Code Ann. § 76–2–305). Abolition of the insanity defense does not mean evidence of mental illness or intellectual disability is irrelevant. Evidence of mental illness or intellectual disability can be used as a failure of proof defense to raise a reasonable doubt that the defendant had the mens rea for the crime.

The insanity defense is not enshrined in the constitution. Thus, it is not unconstitutional to abolish the defense. In *Clark v. Arizona,* 548 U.S. 735, 749 126 S. Ct. 2709 (2006), the Supreme Court wrote, "History shows no deference to *M'Naghten* that could elevate its formula to the level of fundamental principle, so as to limit the traditional recognition of a State's capacity to define crimes and defenses." (*See also, State v. Bethel*, 275 Kan. 456, 66 P.3d 840 (2003); *State v. Korell*, 213 Mont. 316, 690 P.2d 992 (1984); *State v. Herrera*, 895 P.2d 359 (Utah 2005)).

Before leaving the insanity defense, it is important to mention the so-called Product Rule. The product rule originated in New Hampshire in 1871, and remains the law in the Granite State. In 1954, the United States Court of Appeals for the District of Columbia's adopted the product rule in *Durham v. United States*, 214 F.2d 862 (D.C. Cir. 1954). *Durham* ruled a defendant "is not criminally responsible if his unlawful act was the product of a mental disease or defect." (214 F.2d at 874–875). The product rule proved unworkable in practice, and the D.C. Circuit abandoned the rule in 1972 in *United States v. Brawner*, 471 F.2d 969 (D.C. Cir. 1972), in favor of the Model Penal Code approach.

Today, the product rule is used in New Hampshire and the Virgin Islands. (*Petric v. People*, 61 V.I. 401 (2014)).

F. PROCEDURE FOR INSANITY DEFENSE

States differ in procedures for the insanity defense. Generally, a defendant intending to rely on the defense must give advance notice to the prosecution and the court. A judge appoints one or more psychiatrists or psychologists to evaluate the defendant, and testify at trial.

A number of states bifurcate trial when insanity is at issue. In the first phase of trial, defendant is presumed to be sane, and the jury decides guilt or innocence. If the defendant is convicted at phase one, the case moves to phase two, and the jury hears evidence on the insanity defense. (*See People v. Mills*, 55 Cal. 4th 663, 147 Cal. Rptr. 3d 833 (2012); *Jackson v. United States*, 76 A.3d 920 (D.C. 2013); *State v. Anderson*, 357 Wis. 2d 337, 851 N.W.2d 760 (2014)).

G. BURDEN OF PROOF FOR INSANITY DEFENSE

A defendant is presumed sane. (*Clark v. Arizona,* 548 U.S. 735, 126 S. Ct. 2709 (2006); *Medina v. California*, 505 U.S. 437, 112 S. Ct. 2572 (1992); *McAfee v. State*, 467 S.W.3d 622 (Tex. Ct. App. 2015)).

Insanity is an affirmative defense. The defendant must offer evidence of insanity. This requirement is called the burden of producing evidence, or the burden of going forward with evidence. If the defendant fails to meet this burden, then the insanity defense is not "in the case," and is not an option for the jury to consider. The judge will not instruct the jury on the defense.

Assuming the defendant meets the burden of producing evidence of insanity, the next question is; which side has the burden of proof regarding insanity? In many states, the defendant has the burden of proving insanity by a preponderance of the evidence or clear and convincing evidence. (*McAfee v. State*, 467 S.W.3d 622 (Tex. Ct. App. 2015) (preponderance of the evidence); *State v. Anderson*, 357 Wis. 2d 337, 851 N.W.2d 760 (2014)). In Federal Court, and some states, the defendant must prove insanity by clear and convincing evidence. (18 U.S.C. § 17(b); *State v. Calin*, 692 N.W.2d 537 (S.D. 2005)). In about a dozen states, once the defense meets its burden of production, the prosecution has the burden of disproving insanity beyond a reasonable doubt. (*See Clark v. Arizona,* 548 U.S. 735, 126 S. Ct. 2709 (2006)).

H.   EXPERT TESTIMONY AND INSANITY DEFENSE

Expert testimony from mental health professionals plays a vital role in the insanity defense. When a defendant raises the defense, a judge appoints psychiatrists or psychologists to evaluate the defendant and testify at trial. Additional experts may testify.

A defendant who intends to rely on the insanity defense may request the trial court to appoint a mental health professional to evaluate the defendant and testify for the defense. In *Ake v. Oklahoma*, 470

U.S. 68, 105 S. Ct. 1087 (1985), the Supreme Court decided that the Constitution sometimes requires such appointment. The Court wrote:

> When the defendant is able to make an *ex parte* threshold showing to the trial court that his sanity is likely to be a significant factor in his defense, the need for the assistance of a psychiatrist is readily apparent. It is in such cases that a defense may be devastated by the absence of a psychiatric examination and testimony; with such assistance, the defendant might have a reasonable chance of success. In such circumstances, where the potential accuracy of the jury's determination is so dramatically enhanced, and where the interests of the individual and the State in an accurate proceeding are substantial, the State's interest in its fisc must yield.

> We therefore hold that when a defendant demonstrates to the trial judge that his sanity at the time of the offense is to be a significant factor at trial, the State must, at a minimum, assure the defendant access to a competent psychiatrist who will conduct an appropriate examination and assist in evaluation, preparation, and presentation of the case. (470 U.S. at 82–83).

There is no psychological test that determines whether someone meets the insanity defense. The fact that a defendant has a DSM–5 diagnosis is not enough. Gary Melton and his colleagues write, "[A] diagnosis, standing alone, is virtually useless to the legal system." (Gary B. Melton, John Petrila, Norman

G. Poythress & Christopher Slobogin, *Psychological Evaluations for the Courts*, p. 243 (2d ed. 1998)).

A psychological evaluation regarding insanity should be comprehensive. In addition to interviewing the defendant, the mental health professional contacts collateral sources to shed light on the defendant's mental condition at the time of the offense.

With the insanity defense, the issue is the defendant's mental state *at the time of the offense.* There is no gainsaying the difficulty of reconstructing a person's mental state months or years earlier, when events occurred. Mental health professionals cannot be certain what was going through a defendant's mind—what the defendant thought, believed, intended—when the defendant acted. Gary Melton and his colleagues write, "Clinical testimony can be useful here, but only to the extent the clinician sticks to providing informed speculation about the defendant's judgment, concentration, focus of attention, interpersonal functioning, and other aspects of experience at this particular point in time." (Gary B. Melton, John Petrila, Norman G. Poythress & Christopher Slobogin, *Psychological Evaluations for the Courts*, p. 243 (2d ed. 1998)). The Rhode Island Supreme Court grappled with this issue in *State v. Gardner,* 616 A.2d 1124 (R.I. 1992), where the court wrote:

> The trial justice expressed concern over the difficulty and potential unreliability of a retroactive diagnosis. We agree with the trial justice that the process of diagnosing a

defendant after a crime and relating that diagnosis back to the time of the offense is an elusive undertaking. In a meta-physical sense it may be impossible to know the mental state of the defendant at the time of the criminal conduct. Absolute scientific certainty, however, is not the standard for the admissibility of expert testimony. Whatever judicial skepticism may exist regarding psychiatric science is best resolved through the factfinder's determining the credibility and weight to be given the expert's testimony instead of resolving the uncertainty by a total exclusion. The trial justice in this case could have and, indeed, should have addressed the problems posed by [the expert's] testimony by permitting the state to question his testimony on cross-examination. (616 A.2d at 1129).

Expert testimony from a psychologist or psychiatrist that a defendant meets the requirements of the insanity defense can go a long way with jurors, especially if the expert couches the opinion in the language of the applicable defense. Thus, the expert might testify, "The defendant's mental illness is a disease of the mind. Due to his mental illness, at the time of the act, the defendant did not know the nature and quality of the act he did, and he did not know that it was wrong."

Worried that expert testimony that uses the language of the insanity defense carries too much weight with jurors, Congress amended Federal Rule of Evidence 704 to provide, "In a criminal case, an expert witness must not state an opinion about whether the defendant did or did not have a mental state or condition that constitutes an element of the crime charged or of a defense. Those matters are for the trier of fact." (Fed. R. Evid. 704(b)). Rule 704(b) is discussed in Chapter 3, in the subsection on testimony on ultimate issues.

It is worth taking a moment to explain why Congress amended Rule 704. In 1981, John Hinckley shot and nearly killed President Ronald Reagan. Hinckley was trying to impress actress Jodi Foster, and thought killing the Present would do the trick. At trial, Hinckley relied on the insanity defense. Numerous experts testified for and against Hinckley. The jury found Hinckley not guilty by reason of insanity. Congress, and many in the nation, were outraged that Hinckley "got away with it." (He didn't; Hinckley is still confined to St. Elizabeth's hospital in Washington, D.C.). In response to the verdict, Congress amended Rule 704 to limit expert testimony.

Under Rule 704(b), experts should not state opinions in the language of the law. Rather, they should describe the defendant's mental functioning, symptoms, and thought processes.

Rule 704(b) applies outside the context of the insanity defense. Thus, the rule prohibits a mental health professional from offering an opinion that a defendant lacked the capacity to form specific intent. (*See, e.g., United States v. Christian*, 749 F.3d 806 (9th Cir. 2014)).

Although expert testimony plays a central role in insanity defense trials, the jury is not bound by expert testimony. The Wisconsin Supreme Court observed in *State v. Kucharski*, 866 N.W.2d 697 (Wis. 2015), "A trier of fact is not required to accept the opinion of an expert, even if uncontradicted." The Indiana Supreme Court's decision in *Satterfield v. State*, 33 N.E.3d 344 (Ind. 2015), makes the point. The defendant killed his mother and burned down her home. At trial, he raised the defenses of insanity and guilty but mentally ill. There was expert and lay testimony. The jury found defendant guilty, and rejected the mental illness defenses. The Supreme Court wrote:

There was conflicting evidence on whether Satterfield was insane or guilty but mentally ill. In these situations, we let jurors—not courts—weigh the evidence and assess witness credibility. . . . The jury's right to determine the facts allows jurors to disbelieve expert testimony of a defendant's insanity or mental illness and rely instead on other sufficient probative evidence from which a conflicting inference of sanity or mental illness can reasonably be drawn. Demeanor evidence, lay opinion testimony, and the circumstances of the crimes are just a few examples of the additional evidence that juries may consider and use to either accept or reject expert testimony—even when the expert testimony is unanimous.

I.   TEMPORARY INSANITY

Some states recognize a partial defense called temporary insanity. In Texas, for example, voluntary intoxication is not a defense, but evidence of intoxication may be admissible as evidence of "temporary insanity" to mitigate punishment. (*Johnson v. State*, 452 S.W.3d 398 (Tex. Ct. App. 2014)).

J.   GUILTY BUT MENTALLY ILL

In 1975, Michigan became the first state to allow a verdict of guilty but mentally ill. (Mich. Laws. Ann. § 768.36). A number of states followed suit. This verdict is available when a defendant raises the insanity defense, but the jury rejects the defense. The jury can find the defendant not guilty, guilty, or guilty but mentally ill. A defendant found guilty but mentally ill is sentenced, but receives treatment instead of straight prison time. (*See, e.g., Norred v. State,* 773 S.E.2d 234 (Ga. 2015)).

K.   MENTAL ILLNESS AS FAILURE OF PROOF DEFENSE

With a failure of proof defense, the defendant seeks to raise a reasonable doubt that the prosecution proved one or more elements of the crime. Mental illness can be used as a failure of proof defense. (*See* Paul H. Robinson, *Criminal Law Defenses*, vol. 1, § 64, p. 272)). The defendant argues that her mental illness deprived her of the mens rea required for the crime. (*See, e.g., People v. Elmore,* 59 Cal. 4th 121, 325 P.3d 951, 172 Cal. Rptr. 3d 413 (2014)). The

Model Penal Code provides, "Evidence that the defendant suffered from a mental disease or defect is admissible whenever it is relevant to prove that the defendant did or did not have a state of mind that is an element of the offense." (MPC § 4.02(1)). Paul Robinson writes, "The variety of mental disorders that have been admitted to negate an offense element seems to be as broad as they are for the insanity defense." (Paul H. Robinson, *Criminal Law Defenses*, vol. 1, § 64, p. 272, fn.1 (1984)).

The defendant has the burden of producing evidence of mental illness. The prosecution has the burden of proving mens rea beyond a reasonable doubt.

A critical difference between first and second degree murder is premeditation and deliberation. Evidence of mental illness is admissible in most states to prove that the defendant did not premeditate and deliberate, reducing the offense to second degree murder.

In states that recognize the distinction between general and specific intent crimes, mental illness as a failure of proof defense is effective only with specific intent crimes. California recognizes the general intent-specific intent distinction, and in that state, burglary is a specific intent offense. In *People v. Wetmore*, 22 Cal. 3d 318, 583 P.2d 1308, 149 Cal. Rptr. 265 (1978), defendant had a long history of mental illness. Defendant broke into the victim's apartment while the victim was away, and proceeded to live there, wearing the victim's clothes and cooking the victim's food. At his burglary trial, defendant sought to introduce evidence that because of his mental illness, he thought the apartment was his. If he thought the apartment was his, then he lacked the specific intent to commit a felony in the apartment, and was not guilty of burglary. The California Supreme Court ruled the defendant's evidence was admissible.

The four states that abolished the insanity defense—Utah, Idaho, Montana, Kansas—allow mental illness as a failure of proof defense.

Could a state prohibit evidence of mental illness offered to prove lack of mens rea? The United States Supreme Court discussed the issue in *Clark v. Arizona*, 548 U.S. 735, 126 S. Ct. 2709 (2006). Clark suffered from schizophrenia. He shot and killed a police officer. The trial judge ruled that Clark could not rely on evidence of insanity to prove he lacked the mens rea for the crime. The judge cited the Arizona Supreme Court's decision in *State v. Mott*, 187 Ariz. 536, 931 P.2d 1046 (1997), where the Arizona court ruled that expert mental health testimony on battered woman's syndrome was not admissible to prove that the defendant lacked the capacity to form mens rea.

In the U.S. Supreme Court, Clark argued the *Mott* decision's limits on evidence of mental illness violated due process. Rejecting the claim, the Court wrote that Arizona law did not bar *all* evidence of the impact of mental illness on the question of mens rea, and that what evidence it did bar was reasonable, and not an affront to due process. The Court wrote:

> Understanding Clark's claim requires attention to the categories of evidence with a potential bearing on mens rea. First, there is observational evidence in the everyday sense, testimony from those who observed what Clark did and heard what he said; this category would also include testimony that an expert witness might give about Clark's tendency to think in a certain way and his behavioral characteristics. This evidence may support a professional diagnosis of mental disease and in any event is the kind of evidence that can be relevant to show what in fact was on Clark's mind when he fired the gun. . . . [O]bservation evidence can be presented by either lay or expert witnesses.

> Second, there is mental-disease evidence in the form of opinion testimony that Clark suffered a form of mental disease. . . .

> Third, there is evidence we will refer to as capacity evidence about a defendant's capacity for cognition and moral judgment (and ultimately also his capacity to form mens rea). This too, is opinion evidence. . . .

> It is clear that *Mott* itself imposed no restriction on considering evidence of the first sort, the observation evidence. We read the *Mott* restriction to apply, rather, to evidence addressing the two issues in testimony that characteristically comes only from psychologists

or psychiatrists qualified to give opinions as expert witnesses: mental-disease evidence . . . and capacity evidence. . . .

The Supreme Court ruled that when it comes to evidence of mens rea, the Arizona Supreme Court did not run afoul of due process by excluding the second and third types of evidence. Defendants remain free to offer lay and expert testimony in the first category, observation evidence.

L.   DIMINISHED CAPACITY

Several states have a defense called diminished capacity. The details of the defense vary from state to state. Generally, diminished capacity is not a complete defense. In some states, the impact of mental illness causing diminished capacity lowers the seriousness of the offense. (*See Menzies v. State*, 344 P.3d 581 (Utah 2015)). A defendant charged with first degree, premeditated murder, for example, may persuade the jury that his mental illness prevented him from premeditating, thus reducing the offense from first to second degree murder.

Diminished capacity often overlaps the impact of mental illness on mens rea, discussed above. John Parry observes, "Diminished capacity is found in relatively few jurisdictions and in most instances is not really diminished capacity, but rather the lack of mens rea disguised as diminished capacity. At least 18 states, which claim to have a diminished capacity defense actually are referring to the lack of specific intent with regard to an element of the crime, which is more properly called lack of mens rea." (John

Parry, *Criminal Mental Health and Disability Law, Evidence and Testimony,* p. 138 (2009)).

M. INTOXICATION

At an earlier time, voluntary intoxication was not a defense, it was an aggravating factor, deserving harsher punishment. (*Montana v. Egelhoff,* 518 U.S. 37, 116 S. Ct. 2013 (1996)). During the nineteenth century, intoxication was reformulated into a defense. Today, most jurisdictions allow evidence of voluntary intoxication for two purposes: First, to prove that a defendant charged with first degree, premediated murder, was too intoxicated to premediate, lowering the crime to second degree murder. Second, voluntary intoxication may be so severe that it deprived a defendant of the capacity to form specific intent. Voluntary intoxication is generally not a defense to a general intent crime.

The Model Penal Code (MPC) does not distinguish between general and specific intent offenses. Under the MPC, voluntary intoxication is a defense if "it negatives an element of the offense." (MPC § 2.08(1)).

In Arizona and Montana, voluntary intoxication is not a defense. (*State v. Boyston,* 231 Ariz. 539, 298 P.3d 887 (2013); *State v. Ring,* 374 Mont. 109, 321 P.3d 800 (2014)). Arizona Rev. Stat. § 13–503 provides: "Temporary intoxication resulting from the voluntary ingestion, consumption, inhalation or injection of alcohol, an illegal substance . . . or other psychoactive substances or the abuse of prescribed medications does not constitute insanity and is not a defense for any criminal act or requisite state of mind." Montana Code Ann. § 45–2–203 states: "A person who is in an intoxicated condition is criminally responsible for the person's conduct, and an intoxicated condition is not a defense to any offense and may not be taken into consideration in determining the existence of a mental state that is an element of the offense unless the defendant proves that the defendant did not know that it was an intoxicating substance when the defendant consumed, smoked, sniffed, injected, or otherwise ingested the substance causing the condition." The U.S. Supreme Court ruled Montana's statute does not offend the Constitution. (*Montana v. Egelhoff*, 518 U.S. 37, 116 S. Ct. 2013 (1996)).

If voluntary intoxication renders someone "insane," can the person rely on the insanity defense? The answer is generally no. (*See Berry v. State,* 969 N.E.2d 35 (Ind. 2012)). The Model Penal Code states, "Intoxication does not, in itself, constitute mental disease within the meaning of" the insanity defense. (MPC § 2.08(3)). In *Commonwealth v. DiPadova*, 460 Mass. 424, 951 N.E.2d 891 (2011), the Massachusetts Supreme Judicial Court explained:

> Voluntary consumption of alcohol or drugs, intoxication and even alcoholism or drug addiction do not qualify as mental diseases or defects in the [insanity defense]; as a result, a defendant whose lack of substantial capacity is due solely to one of these conditions, and not to any mental disease or defect, is criminally responsible.

Conversely, where a defendant's mental disease or defect, by itself, causes a lack of substantial capacity, the defendant's consumption of alcohol or drugs does not lead to forfeiture of an otherwise valid defense of lack of criminal responsibility. This is true even where that consumption or intoxication may exacerbate or aggravate the symptoms of the mental condition, and even where the defendant knows such aggravation may result, so long as the defendant already lacked criminal responsibility absent the effects of the substances. The legally relevant question is not whether the defendant consumed alcohol or drugs, but what was the cause of his loss of substantial capacity: the consumption or the mental condition?

In other circumstances, a defendant's mental disease or defect may interact with alcohol or drugs in such a way as to push the defendant "over the edge" from capacity into incapacity (*i.e.*, from criminal responsibility into criminal irresponsibility). In such cases, where the combination of alcohol or drug consumption and a mental disease or defect causes a defendant who previously was criminally responsible to become criminally irresponsible, lack of criminal responsibility is established even if voluntary consumption of alcohol or other drugs activated or intensified the mental illness, *unless* the defendant knew or had reason to know that the alcohol or drugs would have that effect. (951 N.E.2d at 897–898, emphasis in original).

In *State v. Anderson*, 357 Wis. 2d 337, 851 N.W.2d 760 (2014), the Wisconsin Supreme Court ruled that "one who mixes prescription medication with alcohol is responsible for any resulting mental state." (851 N.W.2d at 340).

Although acute voluntary intoxication is not a defense, chronic abuse of drugs or alcohol can lead to a permanent "mental disease" called fixed or settled insanity. Settled insanity is an aspect of the insanity defense. (*See Berry v. State,* 969 N.E.2d 35 (Ind. 2012)).

Involuntary intoxication *is* a defense. (*See Jacobson v. State,* 171 So. 3d 188 (Fla. Ct. App. 2015); *People v. Hari,* 300 Ill. Dec. 91, 843 N.E.2d 349 (2006); *People v. Tuduj*, 380 Ill. Dec. 758, 9 N.E.3d 8 (2014)). There are four kinds of involuntary intoxication: (1) Coerced intoxication; (2) Innocent or mistaken intoxication (spiked punch at senior prom); (3) An unanticipated reaction to a drug taken on medical advice; and (4) Pathological intoxication— the defendant knew she was taking a drug, but the reaction was highly excessive. The MPC describes pathological intoxication as, "intoxication grossly excessive in degree, given the amount of the intoxicant, to which the actor does not know he is susceptible." (MPC § 2.08(5)(c)).

Evidence of involuntary intoxication is admissible to disprove general and specific intent. (*Commonwealth v. Okoro*, 471 Mass. 51, 26 N.E.3d 1092 (2015)). In some states, involuntary intoxication is a form of insanity defense (*e.g.*, Illinois). In other states, insanity and involuntary intoxication are separate defenses.

Involuntary intoxication cases are uncommon. (*See People v. Scott*, 146 Cal. App. 3d 823, 194 Cal. Rptr. 633 (1983) (spiked punch led to psychosis)). An interesting example is *United States v. MacDonald*, 73 M.J. 426 (C.A.A.F. 2014). A nineteen-year-old soldier with a completely clean record—an Eagle Scout before enlisting—wanted to quit smoking. An Army doctor prescribed Chantix, a medication intended for this purpose. Not long after starting Chantix, the soldier started having strange thoughts, including thoughts of killing someone. Without provocation, the soldier took a knife and stabbed another soldier some fifty times, killing him. The Court of Appeals for the Armed Forces held that the trial judge erred by refusing to give jury instructions on involuntary intoxication.

N.   COMPETENCE TO STAND TRIAL

A person is competent to stand trial if the person is able to understand the charges and assist defense counsel. (*Dusky v. United States*, 362 U.S. 402, 80 S. Ct. 788 (1960)). The Model Penal Code provides, "No person who as a result of mental disease or defect lacks capacity to understand the proceedings against him or to assist in his own defense shall be tried, convicted or sentenced for the commission of an offense so long as such incapacity endures." (MPC § 4.04).

A minor who is accused of juvenile delinquency, like an adult who is charged with crime, has a due process right not to be tried while incompetent. (*In re R.V.*, 61 Cal. 4th 181, 349 P.3d 68, 187 Cal. Rptr. 3d 882 (2015)).

Doubts about competence typically surface when a defense attorney visits a client in jail and sees that the client is seriously mentally ill. Sometimes, family members bring their doubts to the defense attorney's attention. In some cases, a judge or prosecutor raises the issue. In *State v. Driskill*, 459 S.W.3d 412 (Mo. 2015), the Missouri Supreme Court wrote, "A trial court is required to initiate proceedings to investigate the competency of a defendant whenever a reasonable judge in the same situation as the trial judge would experience doubt about the defendant's competency to stand trial." (459 S.W.3d at 423).

When doubts arise about a defendant's competence to stand trial, the judge orders the defendant evaluated by psychologists or psychiatrists. A hearing may be necessary on the issue of competence to stand trial. The evaluators testify. If the defendant is competent, trial proceeds. If the defendant is not competent, the judge puts the prosecution on hold, and orders treatment for the defendant, usually in jail. If treatment restores the defendant to competence, proceedings resume. If treatment is ineffective, states have procedures to release the incompetent defendant or, if the defendant is dangerous, commit the defendant to a psychiatric facility. (*See State v. C.Z.*, 2015 WL 5245135 (Fla. Ct. App. 2015) (interesting case in which the defendant was incompetent to stand trial, and could not be restored to competence, yet did not meet the criteria for civil commitment to a hospital)

A mental health evaluation for competence to stand trial consists of interviews with the defendant. A number of screening tools are available. The Competency Screening Test, for example, is a 22–item sentence completion test that probes the subject's understanding of the legal process. (*See People v. Holt*, 386 Ill. Dec. 776, 21 N.E.3d 695 (2014); *State v. Bostwick*, 296 Mont. 149, 988 P.2d 765 (1999)). The Competency to Stand Trial Assessment Instrument is a semi-structured interview protocol that yields a numeric score. None of the screening tools is perfect. Except for obviously incompetent defendants, there is no substitute for thorough clinical assessment by an experienced mental health professional.

In an effort to restore a defendant to competence to stand trial, may the state medicate the defendant with antipsychotic medications, against the defendant's wishes? In *Sell v. United States*, 539 U.S. 166, 123 S. Ct. 2174 (2003), the Court said yes, "but only if the treatment is medically appropriate, is substantially unlikely to have side effects that may undermine the fairness of the trial, and, taking account of less intrusive alternatives, is necessary significantly to further important governmental trial-related interests." (*See United States v. Loughner*, 672 F.3d 731 (9th Cir. 2012); *State v. Lopes*, 355 Or. 72, 322 P.3d 512 (2014)). The government must prove the need for medication by clear and convincing evidence. (*United States v. Debenedetto*, 757 F.3d 547, 553 (7th Cir. 2014)).

After a defendant is convicted, the *Sell* standard is used if it is necessary to medicate a defendant so that she is competent to be sentenced. (*United States v. Cruz*, 757 F.3d 372 (3d Cir. 2014)).

In a 2014 case that presages an emerging issue, the Indiana Supreme Court considered what to do with a 67–year–old defendant who was incompetent to stand trial because of dementia (*State v. Coats*, 3 N.E.3d 528 (Ind. 2014)).

O.   COMPETENCE TO WAIVE APPEALS

A competent death row inmate may forego further appeals of the death sentence. In *United States v. Lopez*, 783 F.3d 524 (5th Cir. 2015), the Fifth Circuit wrote, "The Supreme Court has elaborated the legal standard we apply to assess the competency of a death row inmate to abandon further appeals of his sentence, namely whether he has capacity to appreciate his position and make a rational choice with respect to continuing or abandoning further litigation or on the other hand whether he is suffering from a mental disease, disorder, or defect which may substantially affect his capacity in the premises. Applying this standard, we have observed that a habeas court must conduct an inquiry into the defendant's mental capacity . . . if the evidence raises a bona fide doubt as to his competency, further noting that the extent and severity of the petitioner's history of mental health problems which have been brought to the court's attention influence the breadth and depth of the competency inquiry required." (783 F.3d at 524).

P. COMPETENCE TO WAIVE MITIGATION EVIDENCE IN CAPITAL TRIAL

Most, but not all, states hold that a competent defendant who is charged with a capital offense can waive the right to present mitigating evidence. (*State v. Johnson*, 401 S.W.3d 1 (Tenn. 2013)).

Q. COMPETENCE TO WAIVE COUNSEL

A defendant generally has the right to waive counsel and represent him or herself. (*Faretta v. California,* 422 U.S. 806, 95 S. Ct. 2525 (1975)). In *Indiana v. Edwards*, 554 U.S. 164, 128 S. Ct. 2379 (2008), the Supreme Court grappled with a mentally ill defendant who was competent to stand trial if he was represented by counsel, but not competent to conduct his trial. The issue before the Court was "whether in these circumstances the Constitution prohibits a State from insisting that the defendant proceed to trial with counsel, the State thereby denying the defendant the right to represent himself." (554 U.S. at 167). The Court ruled, "The Constitution permits judges to take realistic account of the particular defendant's mental capacities by asking whether a defendant who seeks to conduct his own defense at trial is mentally competent to do so. That is to say, the Constitution permits States to insist upon representation by counsel for those competent enough to stand trial under *Dusky* but who still suffer from severe mental illness to the

point where they are not competent to conduct trial
proceedings by themselves." (554 U.S. at 177–178).

R. COMPETENCE TO WAIVE RIGHT TO SILENCE AND ATTORNEY

Suspects in custody must be given the familiar
Miranda warnings before questioning. A suspect can
waive the rights to remain silent and to an attorney,
but such waiver must be voluntary. Mental illness
and intellectual disability are relevant factors in
determining the voluntariness of waiver. It should be
added, however, that many individuals with mental
illness or intellectual disability are capable of
waiving their *Miranda* rights. (*See, e.g.,
Commonwealth v. Mitchell*, 105 A.3d 1257 (Pa.
2014)). The Georgia Supreme Court wrote in *Griffin
v. State*, 285 Ga. 827, 684 S.E.2d 621 (2009), that
mental illness alone does not render a suspect
incapable of making a voluntary statement. (*Accord,
Williams v. State,* 287 Ga. 199, 695 S.E.2d 246 (2010).

S. COMPETENCE TO ENTER A PLEA

A defendant must be competent to enter a plea. In
State v. Garner, 377 Mont. 173, 339 P.3d 1 (2014), the
Montana Supreme Court wrote, "A guilty plea is a
waiver of constitutional rights, and must be a
voluntary, knowing, and intelligent act. ... A
defendant must be mentally competent to enter a
guilty plea. . . . A defendant is competent when he is
able to consult with his lawyer to a reasonable degree
of rational understanding and has a rational as well

as factual understanding of the proceedings against him." (339 P.3d at 180–181).

The judge engages the defendant in a plea colloquy to determine whether the defendant comprehends the rights he is giving up, and the factual basis of the plea. Many defendants who are mentally ill or intellectually disabled are competent to enter a plea following a searching colloquy by the court.

T. VOLUNTARINESS OF CONFESSION

An *in*voluntary statement extracted by police from a suspect is inadmissible pursuant to the Due Process Clause of the Fourteenth Amendment. To evaluate voluntariness, the court considers the totality of the circumstances, including mental illness and intellectual disability. In *People v. Knapp*, 124 A.D.3d 36, 995 N.Y.S.2d 869 (2014), for example, defendant had an IQ of 68. He was highly suggestible, and was interrogated by a detective skilled in getting people to talk. The defendant's confession was not voluntary, and should have been suppressed. In *Colorado v. Connelly*, 479 U.S. 157, 165, 107 S. Ct. 515 (1986), the Supreme Court noted, "[M]ental condition is surely relevant to an individual's susceptibility to police coercion."

U. EFFECTIVE ASSISTANCE OF COUNSEL AND MENTAL ILLNESS DEFENSES

A defendant has a constitutional right to effective representation. (*Strickland v. Washington,* 466 U.S. 668, 104 S. Ct. 2052 (1984)). The Illinois Appellate Court described the *Strickland* standard: "To prevail on a claim of ineffective assistance, a defendant must show both that counsel's representation fell below an objective standard of reasonableness and that there is a reasonable probability that, but for counsel's unprofessional errors, the result of the proceeding would have been different. . . . To establish that trial counsel's performance was deficient, a defendant must overcome the strong presumption that counsel's action or inaction was the result of sound trial strategy. A reviewing court is highly deferential to trial counsel on matters of trial strategy and must make every effort to consider counsel's performance from his perspective at the time, rather than in hindsight." (*People v. Wood*, 384 Ill. Dec. 157, 16 N.E.3d 253, 265 (Ct. App. 2014)).

A defense attorney who fails to adequately investigate the utility of a psychiatric defense may fall below the *Strickland* line. For example, it can be ineffective assistance of counsel to fail to consult experts regarding a defendant's mental functioning, or to secure the defendant's medical records. (*Commonwealth v. Spray,* 467 Mass. 456, 5 N.E.3d 891 (2014). In *People v. Graham*, 129 A.D.3d 860, 11 N.Y.3d 242 (2015), defendant stabbed his former girlfriend nineteen times, killing her. A jury convicted him of murder. The Appellate Division ruled that defense counsel's failure to obtain psychiatric information deprived the defendant of meaningful representation. The court wrote:

> Here, the People's case hinged almost entirely on their ability to prove the defendant's state of mind, and trial counsel undisputedly failed to

take the minimal steps of obtaining the defendant's psychiatric records and having him evaluated by an expert, which were necessary to make an informed decision as to whether or not to present a psychiatric defense. Under the circumstances of this case, the People's argument that, even with the benefit of the evidence trial counsel should have obtained, there is no reasonable chance that a mental disease or defect or [extreme emotional disturbance] defense would have been successful, or that the outcome of the trial would otherwise have been different, misconstrues the central issue in this case. The issue is not whether trial counsel's choice to have certain documents excluded from the record constitutes a legitimate trial strategy, but whether the failure to secure and review crucial documents, that would have undeniably provided valuable information to assist counsel in developing a strategy during the pretrial investigation phase of a criminal case, constitutes meaningful representation as a matter of law.

In many cases, defense counsel has good reasons for *not* putting on a defense of insanity. In *Torres v. State*, 771 S.E.2d 894 (Ga. 2015), for example, defense counsel considered offering the defense. Counsel took the appropriate steps to evaluate the viability of the defense, and discussed the issue with the defendant. Deciding against the defense was not ineffective assistance of counsel. The Georgia Supreme Court wrote, "A strategic choice which is made after thoughtful consideration will generally not support a claim of ineffective assistance of counsel." (771 S.E.2d at 898). (*See People v. Baker*, 390 Ill. Dec. 183, 28 N.E.3d 836 (2015)).

Most allegations of ineffective assistance of counsel in the context of mental illness defenses fail. (*See State v. Burton*, 349 Wis. 2d 1, 832 N.W.2d 611 (2013)).

V.   COMPELLED EXAMINATION

Can a defendant be compelled to submit to examination by a mental health professional retained by the prosecution? Does requiring a defendant to talk to a prosecution expert violate the defendant's Fifth Amendment right to remain silent? In *Estelle v. Smith*, 451 U.S. 454, 101 S. Ct. 1866 (1981), defendant was charged with capital murder. Prior to trial, he submitted to examination by a psychiatrist to determine whether he was competent to stand trial. The competency examination was not mentioned at the guilt phase of the trial. During the penalty phase, however, the prosecution offered testimony from the psychiatrist who conducted the competency examination. The psychiatrist opined that defendant posed a risk of future dangerousness. The Supreme Court ruled that the psychiatrist's testimony violated defendant's right against self-incrimination. The Court wrote, "A criminal defendant, who neither initiates a psychiatric evaluation nor attempts to introduce any psychiatric evidence, may not be compelled to respond to a psychiatrist if his statements can be used against him at a capital sentencing proceeding." (451 U.S. at 468).

In *Kansas v. Cheever*, 134 S. Ct. 596 (2013), the Supreme Court revisited *Estelle*. Defendant shot and killed a deputy sheriff, and shot at but missed other deputies. Charged with capital murder, the defense gave notice that the defendant intended to offer expert testimony that defendant was voluntarily intoxicated when he killed the deputy. The trial judge ordered defendant to submit to a psychiatric examination by psychiatrist Dr. Welner.

At trial, defendant offered expert testimony that defendant's long-term methamphetamine use damaged his brain, and that, at the time of the shooting, defendant was highly intoxicated. In response, the prosecutor offered testimony from Dr. Welner. Defendant's attorney objected on Fifth Amendment grounds because defendant had not agreed to the examination by Dr. Welner. The Supreme Court rejected the Fifth Amendment argument, writing:

> [W]here a defense expert who has examined the defendant testifies that the defendant lacked the requisite mental state to commit an offense, the prosecution may present psychiatric evidence in rebuttal. Any other rule would undermine the adversarial process, allowing a defendant to provide the jury, through an expert operating as proxy, with a one-sided and potentially inaccurate view of his mental state at the time of the alleged crime. . . .

When a defendant presents evidence through a psychological expert who has examined him, the government likewise is permitted to use the only effective means of challenging that evidence: testimony from an expert who has also examined him. (134 S. Ct. at 601).

Estelle applies to *compelled* psychological evaluation. A defendant who voluntarily submits to evaluation has no claim under *Estelle*. (*See United States v. Graham-Wright*, 715 F.3d 598 (6th Cir. 2013)).

Courts continue to grapple with issues related to the Fifth Amendment and psychological evaluation. Take, for example, *State v. Goff*, 128 Ohio St. 3d 169, 942 N.E.2d 1075 (2010), in which defendant shot her estranged husband fifteen times, unloading two guns into his head and chest. Charged with murder, the defendant claimed self-defense. The defense intended to offer expert testimony on Battered Woman Syndrome. The issue before the Ohio Supreme Court was "whether a court order compelling a defendant to submit to a psychiatric examination conducted by a state expert in response to the defendant raising a defense of self-defense supported by expert testimony on battered-woman syndrome violates the defendant's right against self-incrimination." (942 N.E.2d at 1077). The court ruled a court-ordered examination was proper, writing:

[W]e conclude that when a defendant demonstrates an intention to use expert testimony from a psychiatric examination to establish that battered-woman syndrome caused in her a bona fide belief that she was in imminent danger of death or great bodily harm and that her only means of escape was the use of force, *i.e.*, to use testimony on battered-woman syndrome to prove the second element of self-defense, a court may compel the defendant to submit to an examination by another expert without violating the defendant's rights under . . . the Fifth Amendment to the United States Constitution. By putting her mental state directly at issue and introducing expert testimony based upon her own statements to the expert, the defendant opens the door to limited examination by the state's expert concerning battered-woman syndrome and its effect on the defendant's behavior. Courts have inherent authority to preserve fairness in the trial process, and allowing the defendant to present expert testimony on the specific effects of battered-woman syndrome on the defendant while denying the prosecution the ability to introduce such evidence would unfairly handicap the prosecution and prevent the trier of fact from making an informed decision. We thus conclude that the trial court did not err in ordering [the prosecution's expert, Dr. Resnick's] examination of [defendant] in this case. (942 N.E.2d at 1086–1087).

The limitation on a defendant's bedrock constitutional right against self-incrimination must be carefully tailored to avoid any more infringement than is necessary to ensure a fair trial. The paramount concern of fairness of the trial requires only that the state be given the same opportunity to present testimony on battered-woman syndrome as the defendant. When the expert in *Estelle* testified as to matters beyond the purpose of the compelled examination, the court found a violation of the defendant's Fifth Amendment right. The court found that the expert's "role changed and became essentially like that of an agent of the State recounting unwarned statements made in a post arrest custodial setting." (942 N.E.2d at 1087).

We find that Resnick's role changed in this case in a manner similar to the expert's role in *Estelle.* Psychiatric testimony is one thing—testifying about discrepancies regarding the defendant's recitation of facts and questioning the truth of her presentations regarding her own level of fear are more akin to "recounting unwarned statements made in a post arrest custodial setting." . . . (942 N.E.2d at 1087).

We therefore find that Resnick's testimony violated [defendant's] right against self-incrimination. . . . (942 N.E.2d at 1088).

(*See also, People v. Pokovich,* 39 Cal. 4th 1240, 141 P.3d 267, 48 Cal. Rptr. 3d 158 (2006) (the Fifth Amendment prohibited impeaching the defendant's trial testimony with statements defendant made to mental health professional who evaluated defendant's competence to stand trial); *State v. Harris,* 142 Ohio St. 3d 211, 28 N.E.3d 1256 (2015) (reversible error to admit testimony of psychologist who conducted pretrial competency examination of defendant that he was malingering; at trial defendant offered no mental health testimony)).

W. EXPERT TESTIMONY ON BATTERED WOMAN SYNDROME

Intimate partner violence—domestic violence—is a widespread problem. In rare cases, a victim of intimate partner violence kills or assaults her batterer, and is charged with murder or assault. The defendant may claim self-defense.

The elements of self-defense are similar across the United States. First, a person may claim self-defense only if the person was not the first aggressor, who provoked the confrontation. Second, the defender must use reasonable force to defend, that is, force that is proportional to the attack. Deadly force may only be used to repel a deadly attack. Non-deadly force may be used to defend against a deadly or a non-deadly attack. Wayne LaFave defines deadly force as "force (a) which its user uses with the intent to cause death or serious bodily injury to another or (b) which he knows creates a substantial risk of death or serious bodily injury to the other." (Wayne R. LaFave, *Criminal Law,* § 10.04(b), p. 540 (4th ed. 2003)). The Model Penal Code and a number of states allow deadly force to defend against rape or kidnapping. (Model Penal Code § 3.04). Third, the threatened attack must be unlawful. Fourth, the attack must be imminent or under way. Fifth, the defender must honestly (*i.e.*, subjectively) believe in the need for immediate self-defense. Sixth, the defender's belief in the need for self-defense must be objectively reasonable.

In support of a self-defense claim, the defendant may decide to offer expert testimony on the effects of battering, including testimony on Battered Woman Syndrome (BWS). In *In re* Walker, 147 Cal. App. 4th 533, 546, 54 Cal. Rptr. 3d 411 (2007), the California Court of Appeal explained, "Evidence of intimate partner battering and its psychological effects can . . . support a defendant's theory of justifiable homicide or true self-defense by enabling the jury to find the battered woman or man is particularly able to predict accurately the likely extent of violence in any attack, information that could significantly affect the jury's evaluation of the *reasonableness* of defendant's fear for her [or his] life." In *Smith v. State*, 144 P.3d 159 (Okla. Crim. App. 2006), the Oklahoma Court of Criminal Appeals ruled that a defense attorney rendered ineffective assistance of counsel by failing to offer expert testimony on Battered Woman Syndrome.

Battered Woman Syndrome is not itself a defense. (*See Pickle v. State*, 280 Ga. App. 821, 635 S.E.2d 197, 201 (2006); *State v. Stewart*, 243 Kan. 639, 763 P.2d 572, 577 (1988) *State v. Smullen*, 380 Md. 233, 844 A.2d 429 (2004)). As explained by the Missouri Court of Appeals, "While evidence of the battered spouse syndrome is not in and of itself a defense to a murder charge, its function is to aid the jury in determining whether a defendant's fear and claim of self-defense are reasonable." (*State v. Edwards*, 60 S.W.3d 602, 613 (Mo. Ct. App. 2001)).

When a defendant offers expert testimony on the effects of battering, the prosecution may reply with evidence of its own. In *Gonzalez-Valdes v. State*, 834 So. 2d 933 (Fla. Ct. App. 2003), for example, the defendant was charged with murdering her live-in boyfriend. At trial, the defendant claimed self-defense, and presented expert testimony on Battered Woman Syndrome. On rebuttal, the prosecution offered testimony from the victim's ex-wife that during twenty-nine years of marriage, the victim never raised a hand to her. Approving the rebuttal evidence, the Florida Court of Appeals wrote, "This testimony had a direct bearing on the validity of the expert's opinion concerning the defendant's alleged battered woman's syndrome defense." (834 So. 2d at 935).

When a defendant gives notice that she intends to offer expert testimony on the effects of battering, the prosecution may request a court-ordered psychiatric examination of the defendant. (*People v. Gonzales*, 51 Cal. 4th 894, 253 P.3d 185, 213–214, 126 Cal. Rptr. 3d 1 (2011)). In *State v. Hickson*, 630 So. 2d 172, 176 (Fla. 1993), the Florida Supreme Court ruled:

If a defendant decides that she wants to rely on her expert's relating the battered-spouse syndrome to the facts of her case, . . . she waives her right to refuse to submit to an examination by the state's expert. A defendant who takes the stand waives the privilege against compelled self-incrimination. If a defendant were able to rely on her statements being presented to the trier of fact through an expert's testimony, she would, in effect, be able to testify without taking the stand and subjecting herself to the state's questions. Allowing the state's expert to examine a defendant will keep the state from being unduly prejudiced because a defendant will not be able to rely on expert testimony that the state has no effective means of rebutting. . . .

This presents a defendant with the choice of either (1) having her expert testify directly about her case, in which instance the state may have her examined by its expert, or (2) both sides may present the testimony of experts who have not examined the defendant and who will not testify about the facts of her case.

Some battered women claiming self-defense kill in the prototypical self-defense scenario: The woman kills as her batterer attacks her. (*People v. Garcia*, 28 P.3d 340 (Colo. 2001) (woman killed batterer with long-handled ax); *People v. Evans*, 259 Ill. App. 3d 195, 631 N.E.2d 281 (1995) (defendant stabbed husband to death during an attack with his fists); *State v. Addison*, 717 So. 2d 648 (La. Ct. App. 1998) (woman stabbed man in self-defense); *Wooten v. State*, 811 So. 2d 355 (Miss. Ct. App. 2001) (woman claimed she shot her husband during attack); *State v. Sallie*, 81 Ohio St. 3d 673, 693 N.E.2d 267 (1998)).

Other women, however, kill in circumstances where the need for self-defense is not obvious to someone who has not walked in the woman's shoes. (*State v. Smullen*, 380 Md. 233, 844 A.2d 429 (2004); *State v. Edwards*, 60 S.W.3d 602, 606 (Mo. Ct. App. 2001)). In cases where the need for self-defense is not obvious, jurors may conclude that the woman did not honestly believe she needed to defend herself. Even if the jury concludes her belief in the need for self-defense was honest, the jury may conclude that her belief was unreasonable. For example, a woman who has suffered years of abuse may shoot the batterer when he clenches his fist or "gets that look in his eye." In *State v. Hundley*, 236 Kan. 461, 693 P.2d 475, 479 (1985), for example, the deceased had savagely beaten and threatened his wife for years. Finally, she managed to leave her batterer, but he went to her motel room and broke in. On prior occasions, the deceased had threatened the defendant with beer bottles. In the motel room, the deceased threatened the defendant as he toyed with a beer bottle. The Supreme Court wrote, "Carl's threat was no less life-threatening with him sitting in the motel room tauntingly playing with his beer bottle than if he were advancing toward her."

Because of her experience with violence, a victim of chronic domestic violence understands that she is about to be assaulted. To the average juror, however, the batterer's conduct seems innocuous—hardly an imminent attack. The woman's deadly response appears far out of proportion to the batterer's behavior. Jurors may conclude that the woman did not believe she needed to defend herself, or that her belief was unreasonable. Expert testimony on the effects of battering helps jurors "get inside the head" of the battered woman, to understand the subtle clues of impending violence she knows too well.

But how far inside the head of a battered woman may an expert go? May an expert venture an opinion about what a woman was thinking when she pulled the trigger? The California Court of Appeal grappled with this issue in *People v. Erickson,* 57 Cal. App. 4th 1391, 67 Cal. Rptr. 2d 740 (1997). Defendant, Deborah Erickson, was tried for the murder of her abusive husband. The batterer had a long history of brutalizing and terrorizing Erickson. On the fatal night, the batterer beat and sexually assaulted Erickson and threatened to kill her. After the batterer fell asleep, Erickson went to her son's home, where the two decided to kill the batterer. They returned to Erickson's home, and the son shot the batterer as he slept.

California law provides that expert testimony on the effects of battering is admissible to shed light on "the physical, emotional, or mental effects [of battering] on the beliefs, perceptions, or behavior of victims of domestic violence." (Cal. Evid. Code § 1107(a)). Yet, California law also states, "In the guilt phase of a criminal action, any expert testifying about a defendant's mental illness, mental disorder, or mental defect shall not testify as to whether the defendant had or did not have the required mental states." (Cal. Penal Code § 29. *See also* Fed. R. Evid 704(b)). The trial judge ruled that Erickson's expert witnesses would be permitted "to testify with regard to battered woman's syndrome, including its physical, emotional, and/or mental effects on [Erickson's] beliefs, perceptions, or behavior. [The judge ruled, however, that the defense] expert will not be [permitted] to testify as to what [Erickson's] belief was or wasn't." (57 Cal. App. 4th at 1396). Erickson was convicted, and the Court of Appeal affirmed. The appellate court ruled that the trial judge properly excluded expert testimony on Erickson's state of mind on the night her batterer died.

Cases in which the need for self-defense is *not* obvious fall roughly into two categories: confrontation cases and non-confrontation cases. In confrontation cases, the overt conduct of the batterer does not look to an outsider like the prototypical imminent attack that justifies self-defense. Yet, in the context of a particular violent relationship, an attack may well be imminent or underway. Expert testimony on the effects of battering helps the jury understand the situation from the woman's perspective. For example, the expert may help the jury understand how a battered woman picks up subtle clues of impending violence that are not obvious to outsiders.

The non-confrontation scenario is typified by the woman who shoots her batterer while he sleeps, watches TV, or engages in other conduct that cannot realistically be construed as an imminent attack on the woman. In *State v. Stewart*, 243 Kan. 639, 763 P.2d 572, 579 (1988), the Kansas Supreme Court wrote, "We must, therefore, hold that when a battered woman kills her sleeping spouse when there is not imminent danger, the killing is not reasonably necessary and a self-defense instruction may not be given. To hold otherwise in this case would in effect allow the execution of the abuser for past or future

acts and conduct." (*See also, State v. Norman*, 324
N.C. 253, 378 S.E.2d 8 (1989); *Commonwealth v.
Grove*, 363 Pa. Super. 328, 526 A.2d 369 (1987)
(defendant, with assistance from her daughter, shot
and killed defendant's sleeping spouse)).

Courts are generally unsympathetic to claims of
self-defense in non-confrontation cases. In *State v.
Smith*, 198 W. Va. 441, 481 S.E.2d 747 (1996), for
example, defendant killed her abusive husband as he
slept on a couch. Prior to shooting the batterer,
defendant took her children outside. Defendant
reentered the home and had her 16-year-old son aim
a rifle at the batterer while she steadied the barrel.
The teenager pulled the trigger but the gun misfired.
The batterer did not wake up. Defendant and her son
reloaded the rifle, held it as before, and shot the
batterer as he slept. On these facts, the trial judge
refused to instruct the jury on self-defense, and the
West Virginia Supreme Court affirmed. In a similar
case, *Commonwealth v. Grove*, 363 Pa. Super. 328,
526 A.2d 369 (1987), defendant, aided by her
daughter, shot and killed her sleeping husband. The
Pennsylvania appellate court wrote, "We find that
self-defense was not properly at issue because there
was no evidence presented to establish that appellant
reasonably believed that she or any other person was
in imminent danger of death or serious bodily injury
on the present occasion when the deadly force was
used." (526 A.2d at 372).

In a few cases, battered women hired "hit men" to
kill batterers, and then attempted to claim self-
defense. Courts reject such claims. (*Varner v. Stovall*,

500 F.3d 491 (6th Cir. 2007); *Anderson v. Goeke*, 44 F.3d 675 (8th Cir. 1995); *People v. Yaklich*, 833 P.2d 758 (Col. Ct. App. 1992); *State v. Anderson*, 785 S.W.2d 596 (Mo. Ct. App. 1990); *State v. Martin*, 666 S.W.2d 895 (Mo. Ct. App. 1984); *State v. Leaphart,* 673 S.W.2d 870 (Tenn. Crim. App. 1983)).

X. SENTENCING

At sentencing, judges often consider mitigating evidence, including evidence of mental illness or intellectual disability that reduces the defendant's culpability. In *Archer v. State*, 689 N.E.2d 678 (Ind. 1998), for example, the defendant pleaded guilty but mentally ill to attempted murder and other felonies. The trial judge sentenced him to prison for 165 years. On appeal, the Indiana Supreme Court ruled that the sentencing judge did not give sufficient weight to defendant's long history of mental illness. In light of this mitigating evidence, the Supreme Court lowered the sentence to just 125 years.

In a twist on the norm, in *Mitchell v. United States*, 790 F.3d 881 (9th Cir. 2015), a defense attorney decided *not* to offer evidence of the defendant's mental illness during the penalty phase of a murder trial. On appeal, defendant argued the attorney's decision was deficient, but Ninth Circuit disagreed. The attorney had legitimate strategic reasons for the decision. The attorney's strategy was to emphasize the reasons to preserve the defendant's life, rather than focus on his mental illness.

In the penalty phase of death penalty cases, defendants routinely present evidence of mental disability in an effort to persuade jurors to vote against death. (*See, e.g., Fletcher v. State*, 168 So. 3d 186 (Fla. 2015)).

In *Atkins v. Virginia,* 536 U.S. 304, 122 S. Ct. 2242 (2002), the Supreme Court ruled that the death penalty is not appropriate for mentally retarded criminals. In *Dickerson v. State*, 175 So. 3d 8 (Miss. 2015), the defendant, who was not mentally retarded, ruthlessly murdered the mother of his child. He was sentenced to death. On appeal to the Mississippi Supreme Court, the defendant tried to convince the court to extend *Atkins v. Virginia* to prohibit the death penalty for the mentally ill. The Mississippi court declined the invitation. (*Accord, Ripkowski v. Thaler*, 438 Fed. Appx. 296 (5th Cir. 2011)).

CHAPTER 5

CIVIL COMMITMENT AND OTHER CIVIL MATTERS

No right is more precious than freedom, and no act of government strikes a deeper nerve than depriving people of freedom. Citizens with mental illness share the passion for freedom, yet some people with serious mental illness cannot live safely in the community. Some are dangerous to themselves. Others are dangerous to others. The law of civil commitment seeks a balance between freedom, on one hand, and the government's interest in helping the ill and protecting the innocent, on the other. (*See* Michael Perlin, *Mental Disability Law: Civil and Criminal,* vol. 1 (2d ed. 1998)).

Civil commitment laws are based on two sources of government power. First, police power, which is the authority of government to protect the health, safety, welfare, and morals of the community. Police power authorizes civil commitment of individuals whose mental illness renders them dangerous to others or themselves. Second, *parens patriae* power, which is the authority of government to protect those who cannot protect themselves.

Parens patriae and police power undergird not only civil commitment, but also the law of guardianship, and, to a degree, the juvenile court, child protective services, and adult protective services.

A. SHORT HISTORY OF
INVOLUNTARY COMMITMENT

In the 1800s, a person could be involuntarily committed to an "insane asylum" on the application of a family member, approved by a physician. (Dan Moon, The Dangerousness of the Status Quo: A Case for Modernizing Civil Commitment Law, 20 *Widener Law Review* 209 (2014)). John Parry observes, "Typically, if a judge or the facility administrator, often without any prior medical exam, concurred with the petitioner—usually a husband, father, or guardian—that the proposed mental patient needed treatment, the confinement was almost certain to be authorized. Too often wives were committed for disobeying their husbands; children, for appearing to be different, being defiant, or simply being unwanted." John Parry, *Criminal Mental Health and Disability Law, Evidence and Testimony,* p. 10 (2009). A person committed to an asylum might remain there indefinitely.

In the early 1900s, laws were passed requiring advance judicial approval of involuntary civil commitment. Upon the filing of an application for commitment, a physician examined the person, and testified at a commitment hearing. Commitment was justified on the belief that the seriously mentally ill are incompetent and require treatment.

States built large mental hospitals, housing hundreds of patients. By the 1950s, more than half a million people lived in state mental hospitals. Conditions in some hospitals were deplorable, spurring calls for reform, and exposes such as Ken

Kesey's novel *One Flew Over the Cuckoo's Nest*, made into the 1975 Academy Award winning film starring Jack Nicolson. Another Hollywood critique of early mental hospitals was the 1948 film *The Snake Pit*, starring Olivia de Havilland, and based on a novel by Mary Jane Ward.

Deplorable conditions in mental hospitals were due in part to overcrowding. As well, there was little staff could do to alleviate the suffering of patients. The 1950s saw the discovery of anti-psychotic drugs such as Thorazine. These powerful drugs were, and remain, helpful for many people with mental illness.

By the 1960s, large mental hospitals were criticized as a failure. In 1963, President Kennedy signed the Community Mental Health Centers Act, with the goal of creating community-based outpatient mental health services across the nation, and reducing the need for institutional care. Many large hospitals closed as part of the deinstitutionalization movement of the 1960s and 1970s.

Unfortunately, the best laid plans for deinstitutionalization and treatment in the community did not pan out as hoped. There was never enough money invested in community-based mental health to cope with the onslaught of seriously mentally ill patients leaving mental hospitals. Today, hundreds of thousands of mentally ill individuals are homeless in America, many without access to treatment. Jails and prisons are home to thousands of seriously mentally ill individuals.

B. SHORT-TERM EMERGENCY HOSPITALIZATION

Law allows for emergency, short term (*e.g.*, 72 hour) hospitalization of persons who appear to be seriously mentally ill, and who pose an immediate threat to themselves or others. Typically, these laws allow a police officer to take the person to a hospital. Some states require the officer to consult a mental health professional before hospitalizing the patient. Other states allow an officer to act alone. In addition to police, many states allow physicians and mental health professionals to initiate emergency hospitalization. Usually, a judge is not involved at this stage.

Once at the hospital, the patient is evaluated by a mental health professional. Some patients are allowed to leave following evaluation. Some check themselves into the hospital voluntarily. For patients who need hospitalization, but don't want it, a professional starts the process to civilly commit the patient.

C. LEGAL STANDARDS FOR CIVIL COMMITMENT TO INPATIENT TREATMENT

States have detailed laws governing civil commitment. The procedure starts by filing a petition or similar document in court. The subject of the petition has the right to notice of the proceedings and an adversarial hearing. The individual has the right to an attorney. For individuals who cannot afford an attorney, one is appointed by the court. Generally, the individual has a right to jury trial. The burden of proof is on the government to prove the need for commitment by clear and convincing evidence. (*Addington v. Texas,* 441 U.S. 418, 99 S. Ct. 1804 (1979). *See, e.g., In re Deborah S.*, 26 N.E.3d 922 (Ill. Ct. App. 2015) (evidence did not establish that patient was unable to provide for her basic needs)).

The role of the individual's attorney in civil commitment proceedings is a matter of ethical and practical difficulty. Normally, an attorney is a zealous advocate for the client's wishes. The client, *not* the attorney, makes the critical decisions in litigation. But what is an attorney to do when the client is seriously mentally ill? For example, must an attorney zealously advocate for the wishes of a psychotic client who is opposed to hospitalization, who thinks the FBI is trying to kill him, and who intends to travel to Washington D.C. at the first opportunity, to blow up FBI headquarters?

Individuals subject to civil commitment have the right to effective assistance of counsel. (*In re MH2010–002637,* 228 Ariz. 74, 263 P.3d 82 (Ct. App. 2011); *In re T.A.H.–L.*, 123 Wash. App. 172, 97 P.3d 767 (2004)).

Although the exact wording of civil commitment laws varies from state to state, there is a high degree of uniformity in the legal standard for civil commitment. The government must prove: (1) The individual is mentally ill; (2) As a result of mental illness, the individual poses an immediate threat of substantial harm to the individual or others; and (3) There is no less restrictive alternative to hospitalization that can address the individual's mental health issues.

Dangerousness is at the heart of civil commitment. Yet, as Michael Perlin observes, "No question in the area of the involuntary commitment process has proven to be more vexing than the definition of the word 'dangerousness.'" (Michael Perlin, *Mental Disability Law: Civil and Criminal,* vol. 1, pp. 93–93 (2d ed. 2008)). In some cases, dangerousness is obvious. In others, it is exceedingly difficult to tell whether the legal standard is satisfied.

The assessment of dangerousness proceeds on a case-by-case basis, and can combine testimony from lay and expert witnesses. A lay witness, for example, might, describe a recent assault by the individual, or threats to hurt someone.

Expert testimony is often dispositive in commitment hearings. The expert describes the individual's symptoms and diagnosis. The expert typically offers an opinion on whether the individual is dangerous.

Danger to self is clear when an individual tries to commit suicide. The Wisconsin Supreme Court ruled in *In re Michael H.*, 359 Wis. 2d 272, 856 N.W.2d 603 (2014), that a detailed plan to commit suicide is not necessary to conclude a person is self-dangerous.

A few states add to dangerousness the additional requirement that the person must have engaged in "either recent overt acts or recent expressed treats of violence." (Ga. Code Ann. § 37–3–1).

In addition to commitment for dangerousness to self or others, quite a few states allow commitment of persons whose mental illness renders them gravely disabled (*e.g.*, Arizona, California, Colorado, Connecticut, Idaho, Louisiana, Utah). (*See In re B.O.T.*, 378 Mont. 198, 342 P.3d 981 (2015)). Alaska's definition of gravely disabled is similar to the law in other states, and provides that a person is gravely disabled when, due to mental illness, the individual "is in danger of physical harm arising from such complete neglect of basic needs for food, clothing, shelter, or personal safety as to render serious accident, illness, or death highly probable if care by another is not taken; or will, if not treated, suffer or continue to suffer severe and abnormal mental, emotional, or physical distress, and this distress is associated with significant impairment of judgment, reason, or behavior causing a substantial deterioration of the person's previous ability to function independently." (Alaska Stat. § 47.30.915(7)). Clearly, there is overlap between "gravely disabled" and danger to self.

Iowa has an interesting provision that allows commitment of a mentally ill person who "is likely to inflict serious emotional injury on members of the person's family or others who lack reasonable opportunity to avoid contact with the person with mental illness. . . ." (Iowa Code § 229.1(17)(b)).

D.   RISK ASSESSMENT—PREDICTING DANGEROUSNESS

Predicting dangerousness is central to civil commitment. Yet, the subject is complex and controversial. Michael Perlin writes, "No question in involuntary civil commitment law is more controversial than the extent to which psychiatrists are accurate in their predictions of future dangerousness. . . ." Michael Perlin, *Mental Disability Law: Civil and Criminal,* vol. 1, p. 104 (2d ed. 2008). The American Psychiatric Association states, "While psychiatrists can often identify circumstances associated with an increased likelihood of violent behavior, then cannot predict dangerousness with definitive accuracy. Over any given period some individuals assessed to be at low risk will act violently while others assessed to be at high risk will not." (American Psychiatric Association, *Position Statement on Assessing the Risk of Violence* (2012)).

The traditional approach to risk assessment involves a mental health professional interviewing a subject and drawing on clinical experience to estimate dangerousness. Pure clinical assessment is often unreliable. Gary Melton and his colleagues write, "Clinicians' involvement in violence prediction is extremely controversial. . . . [M]yriad factors limit clinicians' abilities in this area; many have questioned whether mental health professionals' predictions of violent behavior are sufficiently accurate to meet acceptable scientific or legal standards." (Gary B. Melton, John Petrila, Norman

G. Poythress & Christopher Slobogin, *Psychological Evaluations for the Courts,* p. 277 (2d ed. 1998)). Laura Guy and her colleagues add, "[U]nstructured clinical approaches have no association with violence." (Laura S. Guy, Kevin S. Douglas & Stephen D. Hart, Risk Assessment and Communication. In Brian L. Cutler & Patricia A. Zapf (Eds.), *American Psychological Association Handbook of Forensic Psychology,* vol. 1, p. 70 (2015)).

Today, professionals generally supplement clinical interviews with actuarial risk assessment tools. Guy, Douglas and Hart, *supra,* discuss actuarial risk assessment:

At the opposite end of the spectrum from the unstructured clinical approach [to violence assessment] is the actuarial approach. . . . [T]he actuarial approach is seen as "a formal method [that uses] an equation, a formula, a graph, or an actuarial table to arrive at a probability, or expected value, of some outcome." Risk factors are identified through various statistical procedures and are selected based on the strength of their association with violence. . . . Risk factors also may be assigned weights. . . . The hallmark, or defining feature, of the actuarial model of prediction is the derivation and use of reproducible unvarying rules for amalgamating predictive factors. (vol. 1, p. 42).

See also, Douglas Mossman, Allison H. Schwartz & Elise R. Elam, Risky Business Versus Overt Acts: What Relevance Do "Actuarial," Probabilistic Risk

Assessments Have for Judicial Decisions on Involuntary Psychiatric Hospitalization?, 11 *Houston Journal of Health Law and Policy* 365–410 (2012).

Actuarial tools are not a panacea. Research discloses weakness in actuarial assessment. Nevertheless, actuarial assessment is a step forward from pure clinical judgment.

Combining clinical judgment with actuarial tools yields what Guy, Douglas, and Hart, *supra*, call structured professional assessment. Structured assessment is about as accurate at prediction as pure actuarial assessment. Guy and colleagues conclude, "There is no definitive advantage—in terms of predictive accuracy—for either actuarial or structured clinical approaches to assessment of an individual's risk for violence." (vol. 1, p. 53).

Guy and her colleagues are at pains to debunk the myth that risk assessment is worthless. They write, "Decades of research have shown that structured, validated approaches to assessing an individual's risk of violence have on average moderate levels of predictive accuracy. . . ." (vol 1, p. 70).

The U.S. Supreme Court grappled with prediction of dangerousness in death penalty cases. In *Barefoot v. Estelle*, 463 U.S. 880, 103 S. Ct. 3383 (1983), the defendant argued that expert testimony on future dangerousness is too unreliable to be admissible. The defendant was supported by an *amicus* brief filed by the American Psychiatric Association, in which the Association stated, "The unreliability of psychiatric predictions of long-term future dangerousness is by now an established fact within the profession." The Supreme Court majority deflected the position of the Association, and ruled that expert testimony on future dangerousness is admissible. Today, in many kinds of litigation, courts allow expert testimony on dangerousness. It is up to the cross-examiner to point out the weaknesses of such testimony.

E. LEGAL STANDARDS FOR OUTPATIENT COMMITMENT

In addition to civil commitment to inpatient treatment, most states authorize courts to involuntarily commit mentally ill individuals to outpatient treatment. Outpatient commitment is controversial. In 2001, John Monahan and his colleagues wrote, "In many states a take-no-prisoners battle is under way between advocates of outpatient commitment—who call this approach assisted outpatient treatment—and its opponents—who use the term 'leash laws.'" (John Monahan, Richard J. Bonnie, Paul S. Appelbaum, Pamela S. Hyde, Henry J. Steadman & Marvin S. Swartz, Mandated Community Treatment: Beyond Outpatient Commitment, 52 *Psychiatric Services* 1198–1205 (2001)). For a thorough analysis of outpatient commitment, *see* Candice T. Player, Involuntary Outpatient Commitment: The Limits of Prevention, 26 *Stanford Law and Policy Review* 159-237 (2015).

Legal standards for outpatient commitment vary from state to state. Generally, outpatient commitment is allowed for mentally ill patients who require treatment, but who do not require hospitalization. With outpatient commitment, there is less focus on dangerousness, and greater concentration on preventing individuals from deteriorating (decompensating) to the point where they require inpatient care. (*See e.g.,* 405 Ill. Comp. Stat. § 5/1–119.1; N.Y. Mental Hyg. Law § 9.60(C); N.C. Gen. Stat. § 122C–271(a)(1)). Thus, Alabama allows outpatient commitment for mentally ill individuals who will "continue to suffer mental distress and will continue to experience deterioration of the ability to function independently." (Ala. Code § 22–52–10.2). Georgia asks whether outpatient treatment is needed to avoid the risk the individual will imminently become an inpatient. (Ga. Code Ann. § 37–3–1). Hawai'i determines whether the individual "is now in need of treatment in order to prevent a relapse or deterioration which would predictably result in the person becoming imminently dangerous to self or others." (Haw. Rev. Stat. § 334–121(4)). California and Florida require a clinical determination that the individual is unlikely to survive safety in the community without treatment." (Cal. Welfare & Institutions Code § 5346(a)(3); Fla. Stat. § 394.4655(1)(c)). Some states require evidence that the individual has recently received inpatient treatment, or committed dangerous acts. (*e.g.*, Florida, Hawai'i, Louisiana).

F.   RIGHT TO TREATMENT

Is there a legally enforceable right to mental health treatment? Michael Perlin observes that "there was virtually no mention of the idea of a 'right to treatment' in any of the legal literature written prior to 1960." (Michael Perlin, *Mental Disability Law: Civil and Criminal,* vol. 2, p. 6 (2d ed. 1998)). In 1960, Morton Birnbaum, a physician and attorney, published a landmark article in the *Journal of the American Bar Association* titled "The Right to Treatment." (volume 46, pp. 499–505, May, 1960). Morton argued that when the government deprives a person of liberty through civil commitment, the government should provide the treatment needed to restore the person to health. Treatment is the *quid pro quo* for deprivation of liberty. Birnbaum laid the blame for inadequate treatment largely at the feet of politicians, who refuse to appropriate funds to pay for decent treatment. Because legislators fail to fund adequate treatment, Birnbaum urged judges to create a right to treatment. Thus began a long battle for adequate treatment for patients with mental illness and intellectual disability.

An important early right to treatment case was *Rouse v. Cameron,* 373 F.2d 451 (D.C. Ct. App. 1967), written by Judge David Bazelon. Charles Rouse was committed to St. Elizabeth's Hospital in Washington D.C., after being acquitted of an offense on the basis of insanity. Judge Bazelon found a right to treatment in statutory law, thus avoiding the need to decide whether the constitution includes a right to treatment.

The most important right to treatment decision— *Wyatt v. Stickney,* 325 F. Supp. 781 (M.D. Ala. 1971)—was penned in 1971 by Federal District Court Judge Frank Johnson. Judge Johnson ruled that the U.S. Constitution provides a right to treatment for mentally disabled individuals confined in institutions. The right grows out of Fourteenth Amendment substantive due process.

As an aside, readers interested in civil rights may wish to learn about judges Bazelon and Johnson. Both are giants in the field. *See* Robert F. Kennedy, Jr., *Judge Frank M. Johnson, Jr.* (1978); Jack Bass, *Taming the Storm: The Life and Times of Judge Frank M. Johnson, Jr., and the South's Fight Over Civil Rights* (1993); Jack Bass, *Unlikely Heroes: The Dramatic Story of the Southern Judges of the Fifth Circuit Who Transformed the Supreme Court's Brown Decision into a Revolution of Equality* (1981).

The right to treatment issue reached the U.S. Supreme Court in *Youngberg v. Romeo*, 457 U.S. 307, 102 S. Ct. 2452 (1982), dealing with an individual who was profoundly mentally retarded, and living in a state institution. The Court concluded that the constitution requires "the state to provide minimally adequate or reasonable training to ensure safety and freedom from undue restraint." (457 U.S. at 319). The Court did not decide whether there is a broad right to treatment for the mentally retarded or the mentally ill.

After *Youngberg*, efforts to create a right to treatment through constitutional litigation largely stalled. Katie Eyer observes, "Unfortunately, despite its widespread influence, *Wyatt's* legal premises have not fared well in more recent decades. . . . Approximately a decade after *Wyatt*, the Supreme Court addressed for the first time in *Youngberg v. Romeo* the question of whether a substantive due process right to treatment exists. While the Court found that such a right does exist, they found it to be considerably more limited than the right articulated in *Wyatt.* . . . Although some courts have construed *Romeo* broadly or creatively, the decision has unquestionably significantly diminished the utility of due process right-to-treatment arguments." (Katie Eyer, Litigating for Treatment: The Use of State Laws and Constitutions in Obtaining Treatment Rights for Individuals with Mental Illness, 28 *New York University Review of Law and Social Change* 1, at p. 6 (2003)).

If the U.S. Constitution cannot be relied on for a right to treatment, might the mentally ill fare better under state constitutions? Michael Perlin observes, "Surprisingly, there has been virtually no case law on the question of a state constitutional right to treatment on behalf of mentally disabled persons." (Michael Perlin, *Mental Disability Law: Civil and Criminal,* vol. 2, p. 124 (2d ed. 1998)).

There is no constitutional right to treatment in the community. (*Pennhurst State Hospital v. Halderman*, 465 U.S. 89, 104 S. Ct. 900 (1984)). In *Youngberg v. Romeo*, 457 U.S. 307, 317, 102 S. Ct. 2452 (1982), the Supreme Court wrote, "As a general matter, a State is under no constitutional duty to provide substantive services for those within its border." In a similar vein, in *DeShaney v. Winnebago County Department of Social Services* 489 U.S. 189, 195, 109 S. Ct. 998 (1989), the Court wrote, "[N]othing in the language of the Due Process Clause itself requires the State to protect the life, liberty, and property of its citizens against invasion by private actors."

With the recent proliferation of outpatient commitment laws, one may ask: If outpatient treatment is *in*voluntary, does the Due Process Clause require adequate outpatient treatment as the *quid pro quo* for commitment? This question remains unanswered.

G.   RIGHT TO REFUSE TREATMENT

People have the right to refuse medical and psychiatric treatment. (*In re Melanie L.* 349 Wis. 2d 148, 833 N.W.2d 607 (2013)). This right extends to people civilly committed for psychiatric care. (*United States v. Loughner,* 672 F.3d 731 (9th Cir. 2012); *Scott S. v. Superior Court*, 204 Cal. App. 4th 326, 138 Cal. Rptr. 3d 730 (2012)). Except in emergencies, a committed individual cannot be medicated against the person's will absent a court order. (*Smith v. State*, 145 So. 3d 189 (Fla. Ct. App. 2014)). The Alaska Supreme Court wrote in *Myers v. Alaska Psychiatric Institute,* 138 P.3d 238 (2006), "In keeping with most state courts that have addressed the issue, we hold that, in the absence of emergency, a court may not authorize the state to administer psychotropic drugs to a non-consenting mental patient unless the court determines that the medication is in the best interests of the patient and no less intrusive alternative treatment is available." (p. 238). (*See also, Steinkruger v. Miller*, 612 N.W.2d 591 (S.D. 2000) (forced medication statute satisfied due process because it required court to consider less intrusive alternatives before approving forced medication)).

In the prison context, the U.S. Supreme Court, in *Washington v. Harper*, 494 U.S. 210, 110 S. Ct. 1028 (1990) ruled, "[G]iven the requirements of the prison environment, the Due Process Clause permits the State to treat a prison inmate who has a serious mental illness with antipsychotic drugs against his will, if the inmate is dangerous to himself or others and the treatment is in the inmate's medical interest." (494 U.S. at 227).

The right to refuse treatment extends to electroshock therapy (ECT). When an individual's mental illness renders the person incapable of consenting to ECT, a proceeding may started seeking judicial approval of the procedure. (*See Conservatorship of Pamela J.*, 133 Cal. App. 4th 807, 35 Cal. Rptr. 3d 228 (2005); *In the Matter of A.A.*, 381 N.J. Super. 334, 885 A.2d 974 (2005) (good description of electroshock treatment).

H.   RULES OF EVIDENCE AT COMMITMENT HEARINGS

The rules of evidence generally apply at civil commitment hearings. (*Scott S. v. Superior Court*, 204 Cal. App. 4th 326, 138 Cal. Rptr. 3d 730 (2012)). In many states, the psychotherapist-client and physician-patient privileges have limited application in commitment proceedings. (*See In re Winstead*, 67 Ohio App. 2d 111, 425 N.E.2d 943 (1980) (privilege not applicable)).

I.   PERIODIC REVIEW OF COMMITMENT

Decades ago, during the era of large state hospitals housing hundreds of patients, it was common for civilly committed individuals to disappear into institutions, and be forgotten. Today, commitments typically last a set number of days, and must be reviewed on a regular basis. The patient has a right to seek release.

When professionals believe a commitment should be extended, procedures exist to do so. In Wisconsin, for example, "the extension of an involuntary mental health commitment . . . requires the circuit court to find by clear and convincing evidence that the individual is mentally ill and is a proper subject for treatment and that there is a substantial likelihood, based on the subject individual's treatment record, that the individual would be a proper subject for commitment if treatment were withdrawn." (*Mental Health Commitment of James H.,* 364 Wis. 2d 529 (Wis. Ct. App. 2015) (unpublished disposition). *See also, In re T.S.S.,* 121 A.3d 1184 (Vt. 2015)).

J.   CIVIL COMMITMENT OF PERSONS WITH INTELLECTUAL DISABILITY

The DSM–5 uses the term Intellectual Developmental Disorder (IDD) to describe what used to be called mental retardation. Statutes govern the appointment of a conservator or guardian for persons with IDD. Statutes also establish procedures to place persons with IDD in institutions when such persons cannot live independently. (*See Michelle K. v.*

Superior Court, 221 Cal. App. 4th 409, 164 Cal. Rptr. 3d 232 (2013)).

Florida's law is typical. A petition is filed in the appropriate county court, alleging, "The person lacks sufficient capacity to give express and informed consent to a voluntary application for services and lacks the basic survival and self-care skills to provide for the person's well-being or is likely to physically injure others if allowed to remain at liberty." (Florida Stat. § 393.11(2)(c)(4)). Notice is given to the person or her guardian. The court appoints three experts to evaluate the person. The person has the right to an attorney. A hearing is held, and there must be clear and convincing evidence to commit the person to care.

K.   CIVIL COMMITMENT OF CHILDREN

Parents have the right to consent to medical care for their children. (*In re Cassandra C.*, 316 Conn. 476, 112 A.3d 158 (2015)). Does this include the right to admit a child to a mental hospital? Skeptics of unfettered parental authority worry that some parents who are fed up with troublesome teenagers will "dump" children in hospitals to get rid of "the problem." Those favoring parental authority respond that such abuses are rare, and, when they occur, it is important to remember that parents cannot unilaterally admit children to hospital. A mental health professional must agree the child needs hospitalization.

The U.S. Supreme Court waded into this minefield in *Parham v. J.R.*, 442 U.S. 584, 99 S. Ct. 2493 (1979). The Court examined the interests of children, parents, and the state. The Court assumed that children have a constitutionally protected interest in being free from unnecessary bodily restraint, and in not being erroneously labeled mentally ill. Turning to parents, the Court referred to the long line of cases recognizing the importance of parental authority, writing, "Parents generally have the right, coupled with the high duty, to recognize and prepare [their children] for additional obligations." (442 U.S. at 602). The Court noted, "Most children, even in adolescence, simply are not able to make sound judgments concerning many decisions, including their need for medical care or treatment. Parents can and must make those judgments." (Id. at 603). As for the government, the state has an interest in conserving scarce mental health recourses, and not wasting those resources where they are not needed.

The Court ruled that although parents play a dominant role in deciding whether hospitalization is necessary, "parents cannot have absolute and unreviewable discretion to decide whether to have a child institutionalized." (Id. at 604). The Court ruled that an adversarial commitment hearing, required for adult commitments, is not constitutionally required for children. Indeed, the Court worried that formal hearings would discourage parents from getting help for their children. The Court wrote:

> The State in performing its voluntarily assumed mission also has a significant interest in not imposing unnecessary procedural obstacles that may discourage the mentally ill or their families from seeking needed psychiatric

assistance. The *parens patriae* interests in helping parents care for the mental health of their children cannot be fulfilled if the parents are unwilling to take advantage of the opportunities because the admission process is too onerous, too embarrassing, or too contentious. It is surely not idle to speculate as to how many parents who believe they are acting in good faith would forgo state-provided hospital care if such care is contingent on participation in an adversary proceeding designed to probe their motives and other private family matters in seeking the voluntary admission. (Id. at 605).

The Supreme Court ruled that due process is satisfied so long as there is "some kind of inquiry by a neutral factfinder to determine that hospitalization is required. The factfinder can be a mental health profession, and need not be a judge. No formal hearing is required. "Due process is not violated by use of informal traditional medical investigative techniques." (Id. at 607).

L. SOCIETAL INCENTIVES FOR PATIENTS TO PARTICIPATE IN TREATMENT

Civil commitment is a raw use of government power. With insight typical of his extensive expertise on mental health law, John Monahan discusses other methods employed by society to "leverage" individuals with mental illness into compliance with care and socially acceptable conduct. (John Monahan, Richard J. Bonnie, Paul S. Appelbaum, Pamela S. Hyde, Henry J. Steadman & Marvin S.

Swartz, Mandated Community Treatment: Beyond Outpatient Commitment, 52 *Psychiatric Services* 1198–1205 (2001)).

Monahan and his colleagues describe "money as leverage." Over one million people with mental disorders receive disability benefits—Supplemental Security Income or Social Security Disability. Many of these individuals have a representative payee who receives the money on behalf of the recipient. Monahan writes, "In a majority of representative payee programs, some relationship exists between treatment adherence and receipt of funds; in a substantial minority of programs this relationship approaches quid pro quo status." (p. 1199).

Monahan describes "housing as leverage." The government provides housing in the community for many disabled individuals. However, the largess comes with strings attached. "Many people who have mental disorders appear to be prepared to accept services if such a trade-off is required in order for them to obtain the housing they want." (p. 1199).

Monahan describes "avoidance of jail as leverage." Many mentally ill individuals who are charged with minor offensees are willing to accept treatment to avoid jail. (p. 1200).

Many mentally ill individuals will accept outpatient commitment as a more attractive alternative than inpatient care. (p. 1200).

One can, indeed, should, debate the morality of "leveraging" people into compliance with mental health treatment. Is it right to say to someone, "Take your medication and go to treatment or lose your money and your apartment?" Reasonable minds differ on the use of such "incentives." Needless to say, there are cases of overreaching and abuse. Those with a civil liberties bent recoil from the coercion that is inherent in leverage. Those with more paternalistic leanings view incentives as humane ways to help disabled individuals live in the community with dignity.

M.   CIVIL COMMITMENT OF SEX OFFENDERS

Some dangerous sex offenders are not safe at large. Yet, when their prison term expires, they are entitled to release. Most such offenders cannot be committed for traditional psychiatric treatment because they do not have the mental illness required for civil commitment.

In the middle of the twentieth century, a number of states had laws that permitted involuntary commitment of dangerous sex offenders. In the 1970s and 1980s, those laws fell into disuse. In the 1990s, however, states resurrected laws allowing involuntary civil commitment of sexually violent predators.

In 1997, the U.S. Supreme Court upheld the constitutionality of Kansas' sexual predator commitment law. (*Kansas v. Hendricks,* 521 U.S. 346, 117 S. Ct. 2072 (1997)). State courts have upheld similar laws.

In 2002, the U.S. Supreme Court revisited the Kansas law, and ruled that in commitment proceedings, substantive due process requires the state to prove that the sexually dangerous individual has some degree of inability to control himself. (*Kansas v. Crane*, 534 U.S. 407, 122 S. Ct. 867 (2002)). The New York Court of Appeals explained in *State v. Floyd Y.*, 979 N.Y.S.2d 240, 2 N.E.3d 204, 209 (2013), "A state may only use civil process to confine a sex offender for treatment for a mental abnormality that makes it difficult, if not impossible, for the person to control his or her dangerous behavior."

In sex offender commitment proceedings, the principal issue is the likelihood the offender will re-offend in the future. Past is prologue, and the best evidence of future offending is past offending. Thus, in commitment proceedings, the offender's history of offending is admissible.

Mental health professionals who evaluate individuals in sex offender commitment proceedings use clinical judgment and actuarial instruments to assess the risk of re-offending. (*In re Commitment of Bohannan*, 388 S.W.3d 296 (Tex. 2012) (expert used Static–99)). The Washington Supreme Court observed, "There are two broad approaches to conducting risk assessments: clinical judgment or actuarial assessment. The clinical approach requires evaluators to consider a wide range of risk factors and then form an overall opinion concerning future dangerousness. The actuarial approach evaluates a limited set of predictors and then combines these variables using a predetermined, numerical weighting system to determine future risk of re-offense which may be adjusted (or not) by expert evaluators considering potentially important factors not included in the actuarial measure." (*In re Detention of Thorell*, 149 Wash. 2d 724, 72 P.3d 708, 724 (2003)).

The tragic facts of *State Department of Hospitals v. Superior Court*, 61 Cal. 4th 339, 188 Cal. Rptr. 3d 309 (2015), illustrate the importance, and limitations, of risk assessment. Gilton Pitre was scheduled to be paroled from prison. Before his release, the State Department of Mental Health evaluated Pitre to determine whether he should be civilly committed as a dangerous sexual predator. The evaluation did not conform with all aspects of state law. The Department did not request Pitre's commitment. Four days after leaving prison, Pitre raped and murdered a fifteen-year-old girl. The victim's sister sued the Department of Mental Health, but the California Supreme Court ruled the Department's failure to comply with every aspect of the evaluation process was not the proximate cause of the rape and murder.

N. VOLUNTARY HOSPITALIZATION

Most people in mental hospitals are *not* committed; they are in the hospital voluntarily. Many individuals with serious mental illness are competent to consent to hospitalization and treatment. Others, however, are so ill or out of touch with reality that they lack capacity to consent to hospitalization. For these individuals, who holds the key to admission? It would be quite a Catch-22 to deny hospital care to someone who needs it, but whose illness deprives the person of the ability to consent to care.

Some people who lack capacity to consent to care could enter the hospital through civil commitment. Yet, civil commitment is time consuming, expensive, and adversarial. Not to mention, many people who need inpatient treatment do not meet the criteria for involuntary civil commitment.

It does not make sense medically, legally, or humanely, for civil commitment to be the only way into the hospital for patients who are too ill to consent to care. States have developed alternatives to civil commitment. In some states, family members can admit ill loved ones to hospital.

A guardian may be appointed, and given authority to consent to hospitalization. (*See Cohen v. Bolduc*, 435 Mass. 608, 760 N.E.2d 714 (2002)). Regarding guardians, Richard Boldt writes, "In a number of states, the law is clear that a guardian may not consent to the ward's admission to a psychiatric hospital, thus requiring the use of the state's involuntary civil commitment process. . . . In other states, it is clear that a guardian may provide the necessary consent for voluntary admission. In a third group of states, the guardian may consent so long as the ward also consents or, in some jurisdictions, does not object. In a fourth group of states, the guardian's authority to arrange for voluntary inpatient care depends on the guardian obtaining specific court authorization, although the substantive standard and procedural requirements for securing such an order may differ from those that govern involuntary commitment." (Richard C. Boldt, The "Voluntary" Inpatient Treatment of Adults Under Guardianship, 60 *Villanova Law Review* 1-52, at pp. 2–3 (2015)).

With the mentally ill, intellectually disabled, and elderly, there is the danger that unscrupulous family members, "friends," or caretakers will "dump" them in institutions and make off their property. Richard Boldt writes, "It is, perhaps, because of the coercive features present within many voluntary mental hospital admissions that state law generally imposes restrictions on the practice that are not ordinarily present in the case of voluntary hospital admission for other healthcare services. State laws typically contain detailed provisions setting out the process by which an individual may elect to enter an inpatient mental health treatment facility, the criteria under which that application for admission is to be assessed by hospital personnel, and the rights and restrictions (particularly on requesting discharge from the hospital) that apply once the voluntary patient is admitted." (Richard C. Boldt, The "Voluntary" Inpatient Treatment of Adults Under Guardianship, 60 *Villanova Law Review* 1, at pp. 10–11 (2015)). When financial exploitation or neglect is suspected, adult protective services is contacted.

O. ADVANCE DIRECTIVES

An advance directive is a legal document, signed while a person is competent, setting forth the person's wishes for medical care if the person becomes incompetent. In some states, a directive is called a power of attorney for health care decisions. Advance directives are often used to help with end-of-life decision making. State laws vary on the details of advance directives. (*See* Karl Menninger, II, Advance Directives for Medical and Psychiatric Care, 102 *American Jurisprudence, Proof of Facts* 3d (2008, 2015)).

Individuals with mental illness can use a psychiatric advance directive. (*See In the Matter of A.A.*, 381 N.J. Super. 334, 885 A.2d 974 (2005)). Beanne Sheetz describes this tool:

> The directive can take several forms. One type, the instructional directive, allows individuals to provide directions about treatments that they would or would not like to receive while they are incapable of making treatment decisions. A second type, a proxy directive, permits individuals to appoint an agent to make decisions for them while they are incapacitated. Another type, the hybrid directive, contains elements of both instructional and proxy directives. A fourth type, the Ulysses directive, is most pertinent to individuals with episodic and insight-impairing issues . . . because it enables them prospectively to bind themselves to treatment and override, in advance, their refusals during acute episodes of their illnesses.

(Breanne M. Sheetz, Note, The Choice to Limit Choice: Using Psychiatric Advance Directives to Manage the Effects of Mental Illness and Support

Self-Responsibility, 40 *University of Michigan Journal of Law Reform* 401, 403 (2007)).

Judy Clausen explains Ulysses directives, "A Ulysses arrangement authorizes doctors to treat the patient during a future episode when the patient lacks capacity even if the episode causes the patient to refuse treatment at that time. A patient who enters a Ulysses arrangement essentially requests doctors to ignore the patient's illness-induced refusals." (Judy A. Clausen, Making the Case for a Model Mental Health Advance Directive Statute, 14 *Yale Journal of Health Policy, Law, and Ethics* 1, p. 4 (2014)).

P.   IMMIGRATION

Federal immigration law states that mental illness posing a danger to persons or property is a ground for inadmissibility.

Individuals in the United States who are subject to removal proceedings have due process rights, although these rights are not the same as rights enjoyed by defendants in the criminal justice system. For example, under *Dusky v. United States*, 362 U.S. 402, 80 S. Ct. 788 (1960), an incompetent defendant in the criminal system cannot be tried. Not so before an immigration judge. The court explained in *Mohamed v. Tebrake*, 371 F. Supp. 2d 1043 (D. Minn. 2005):

Petitioner alleges that the immigration judge violated his right to due process of law when he failed to hold a competency hearing. The Fifth

Amendment due process clause mandates that removal proceedings be fundamentally fair. The law is undeveloped, however, with regard to the particular demands of fundamental fairness in removal proceedings against a potentially incompetent alien. The court therefore looks to the requirements of due process in other similar contexts. In criminal proceedings, the law recognizes an absolute due process right to a competency hearing whenever evidence raises a sufficient doubt about the mental competency of an accused to stand trial. However, this procedural competency principle exists only to ensure that a second, substantive competency principle is not violated. The substantive competency principle holds that due process absolutely prohibits the trial and conviction of a defendant who is, in fact, mentally incompetent.

The substantive competency principle has no corollary in immigration proceedings. Indeed, the law specifically contemplates that removal proceedings may go forward against incompetent aliens and that incompetent aliens may be deported. (371 F. Supp. 2d at 1045–1046).

A federal regulation provides a measure of guidance for immigration judges. The regulation—8 C.F.R. § 1240.4—provides:

When it is impracticable for the respondent to be present at the hearing because of mental incompetency, the attorney, legal representative, legal guardian, near relative, or friend who was served with a copy of the notice to appear shall be permitted to appear on behalf of the respondent. If such a person cannot reasonably be found or fails or refuses to appear, the custodian of the respondent shall be requested to appear on behalf of the respondent.

Although individuals may be represented by counsel at immigration proceedings, the government does not pay for counsel. (Mimi E. Tsankov, Incompetent Respondents in Removal Proceedings, 3 *Immigration Law Advisor* (April, 2009) (U.S. Department of Justice).

Q.   INFLICTION OF EMOTIONAL DISTRESS

Intentional and negligent infliction of emotional distress play important roles in tort litigation. Section 46 of the *Restatement of Torts, Third*, defines intentional infliction of emotional distress as follows: "An actor who by extreme and outrageous conduct intentionally or recklessly causes severe emotional harm to another is subject to liability for that emotional harm and, if the emotional harm causes bodily harm, also for the bodily harm."

Section 47 addresses "negligent conduct directly inflicting emotional harm on another," and provides, "An actor whose negligent conduct causes serious emotional harm to another is subject to liability to the other if the conduct: (a) places the other in danger of immediate bodily harm and the emotional harm results from the danger; or (b) occurs in the course of specified categories of activities, undertakings, or relationships in which negligent conduct is especially likely to cause serious emotional harm."

The California Supreme Court's decision in *Marlene F. v. Affiliated Psychiatric Medical Clinic*, 48 Cal. 3d 583, 770 P.2d 278, 257 Cal. Rptr. 98 (1989), is a leading authority on negligent infliction of emotional distress. The mothers of three children took their sons to the psychiatric clinic for counselling. The children were assigned to a psychologist. The psychologist counselled the mothers and the children. The psychologist sexually abused the boys. When the children disclosed, the mothers confronted the owner of the clinic, who told them the psychologist did nothing illegal, but that he (the psychologist) would no longer treat children.

Two of the mothers sued the clinic and the offending psychologist, claiming that the sexual abuse caused the mothers emotional suffering. The Supreme Court wrote:

> In these circumstances, the therapist, as a professional psychologist, clearly knew or should have known in each case that his sexual molestation of the child would directly injure and cause severe emotional distress to his other patient, the mother, as well as to the patient-child relationship that was also under his care. His abuse of the therapeutic relationship and molestation of the boys breached his duty of care to the mothers as well as to the children. (48 Cal. 3d at 591).

CHAPTER 6

CIVIL LIABILITY OF MENTAL HEALTH PROFESSIONALS

Lawsuits against mental health professionals are relatively uncommon. Yet, the complexity of mental health law and practice, coupled with the serious consequences of error, means the potential for liability cannot be ignored. This chapter addresses civil liability of mental health professionals.

A. MALPRACTICE

The word "malpractice" combines "mal" and "practice." In Latin, "male" means badly. Thus, malpractice literally means bad practice. Claims of malpractice are generally based on negligence. The *Restatement of Torts, Third* defines negligence: "A person acts negligently if the person does not exercise reasonable care under all the circumstances." (§ 3.) The elements of negligence are: (1) Duty of care, (2) Breach of duty, (3) Causation (cause in fact and proximate cause), and (4) Harm.

In malpractice litigation, expert testimony is normally required to establish that a defendant fell below the standard of care. (*Nwaneri v. Sandidge,* 931 A.2d 466, 470 (D.C. 2007); *Texas Home Management, Inc. v. Peavy,* 89 S.W.3d 30 (Tex. 2002)). In rare cases, malpractice is so obvious that expert testimony is not required. As the Louisiana Court of Appeal put it in *Elledge v. Williamson*, 132 So. 3d 432 (La. Ct. App. 2014), "Plaintiff is generally required to produce expert testimony in a medical malpractice action to establish the applicable standard of care and to determine whether that standard was breached, except where the negligence is so obvious that a lay person can infer negligence without the counsel of expert testimony." (p. 438).

The *Restatement of Torts, Third* provides that individuals ordinarily have a duty of due care when the individual's conduct creates a risk of harm to others. (§ 7(a)). Mental health professionals owe a duty of care to clients. As an example, the standard of care dictates that therapists not have sex with clients. When a therapist does so, the behavior falls below the standard of care, breaches the duty owed the client, and is malpractice.

Mental health professionals are not guarantors of success. Thus, mental health professionals are generally not liable when a course of treatment is not effective. "Liability is imposed only if the doctor's treatment decisions do not reflect his or her own best judgment, or fall short of the generally accepted standard of care." (*Park v. Kovachevich*, 116 A.D.3d 182, 982 N.Y.S.2d 75, 81 (2014)). Errors in judgment, as well as mistakes, are not typically malpractice. The standard of care does not require perfection.

B.   PSYCHOTHERAPY

Psychotherapy—talk therapy—is seldom a basis for malpractice liability. There are many theories and techniques of psychotherapy. A competent therapist does not guarantee success.

Liability could attach if a professional restricts treatment to talking, in the face of evidence that something else is needed. For example, if a competent psychotherapist would realize that a client's symptoms point to organic disorder—*e.g.,* dementia, brain tumor—liability could follow the therapist's failure to apprehend the client's condition and make the proper referral. Thus, in *Deasy v. United States*, 99 F.3d 354 (10th Cir. 1996), the plaintiff, a disabled veteran, successfully sued two VA medical centers because VA psychiatrists failed to refer him for treatment of edema, a buildup of fluid in the body.

A therapist might be liable for continuing talk therapy when a competent professional would understand the client has decompensated to the point of needing hospitalization.

There is one area of psychotherapy, as practiced by a small number of therapists in the 1980s and 1990s, that led to lawsuits. Therapist were accused of using highly suggestive techniques to implant in clients false memories of childhood sexual abuse. (*See Johnson v. Rogers Memorial Hospital*, 283 Wis. 2d 384, 700 N.W.2d 27 (2005)).

C.   INFORMED CONSENT

Before medical or psychological treatment begins, the client must consent. (*Canterbury v. Spence*, 464 F.2d 772 (D.C. Cir. 1972)). Consent is only valid if it is informed. (*Barcai v. Betwee*, 98 Hawai'i 470, 50 P.3d 946 (2002)). Treatment without informed consent can constitute malpractice.

To ensure that consent is informed, the client should be informed of: (1) Nature and limits of proposed treatment; (2) Likelihood of successful treatment; (3) Risks and benefits of treatment; (4) Side effects; (5) Alternatives to proposed treatment; (6) Client's right to refuse or terminate treatment; and (7) Extent and limits of confidentiality.

Discussing side effects of medicines is an important part of informed consent. Some medicines used to treat mental illness have powerful side effects, which can be permanent. The most well-known side effect of certain antipsychotic drugs is the neurological disorder called tardive dyskinesia. Sheldon Gelman describes tardive dyskinesia, "The tongue, mouth, and chin are common signs of tardive dyskinesia: the tongue sweeps from side to side, the mouth opens and closes, and the jaw moves in all directions. Fingers, arms and legs may display comparable movements; swallowing, speech or breathing can be affected as well." (Sheldon Gelman, Mental Hospital Drugs, Professionalism and the Constitution, 72 *Georgia Law Journal* 1725 (1984)). Patients who developed tardive dyskinesia have sued mental health providers. (*See Deen v. Pounds*, 312 Ga. App. 207, 718 S.E.2d 68 (2011) (medical malpractice action barred by statute of limitations); *Barclay v. Campbell,* 704 S.W.2d 8 (Tex. 1986)).

When a client is court-ordered for a mental health evaluation, informed consent is often not necessary. Nevertheless, the professional informs the client of the elements of informed consent, and helps the client understand whether and to what extent the client can refuse evaluation.

When a person is not competent to consent to treatment, another person may be appointed to consent on their behalf (*e.g.*, guardian or conservator). In some cases, consent is obtained from a judge.

Informed consent is not required in emergencies, where an individual needs immediate care, but is incapable of consenting, perhaps because the person is unconscious.

Children lack capacity to consent to most medical and psychological care. Parents have authority to consent for their children. When a parent's refusal to consent to care for a child poses a risk of injury or death to the child, a court may overrule the parents and consent to care.

States allow teenagers to consent to some types of care, especially regarding reproductive health and mental health counseling. For example, in California, a minor twelve or older may consent to mental health care. The teen's parents are to be involved unless the provider determines parental involvement would be inappropriate. (Cal. Family Code § 6924). A teenager can consent to medical care related to prevention and treatment of pregnancy. (Cal. Family Code § 6925). A teen can consent to treatment of sexually transmitted disease. (Cal. Family Code § 6926). Finally, a minor who is the victim of rape or sexual assault may consent to medical care and the collection of medical evidence regarding the offense. (Cal. Family Code §§ 6927, 6928).

D.   DISCLOSURE OF CONFIDENTIAL/PRIVILEGED MATTER

Mental health professionals can be sued for improperly disclosing confidential and/or privileged records. (*See* the Discussion of HIPAA in Chapter 2). In *David D. v. Luzio*, 22 A.D.3d 517, 802 N.Y.S.2d 233 (2013), for example, the plaintiff was a minor when it was discovered he sexually abused a younger child. The minor was brought before the juvenile court, and was evaluated by mental health professionals. Later, the mental health professionals devised a mock trial based on the juvenile court case, and performed the mock trial to help other mental health professionals understand juvenile court. Apparently, during performances of the mock trial, the offending minor's name, and that of the other child, was revealed. The minors sued. Although the suit was unsuccessful because the minors did not prove damages, the case illustrates the importance of keeping confidential information—including names—confidential.

Another interesting case is *Gracy v. Eaker*, 837 So. 2d 348 (Fla. 2002). A married couple consulted a mental health professional for help with marital difficulties. According to the couple, during individual sessions with the therapist, each disclosed to the therapist, *in confidence*, extremely private information that they had never revealed to their spouse. The therapist then revealed this information to the other spouse. The couple sued the therapist for emotional distress caused by disclosing the information. The Florida Supreme Court ruled the case could go forward.

E. SUICIDE

No area of mental health practice poses a greater risk of being sued than patient suicide. The New Jersey Supreme Court wrote, "A psychiatrist treating a suicidal patient may have a duty to protect the patient from self-harm." (*Komlodi v. Picciano*, 217 N.J. 387, 89 A.3d 1234, 1247 (2014)). Suicide-related cases generally involve: (1) Suicide by a hospitalized patient, (2) Suicide after a patient is released from the hospital, and (3) Suicide by outpatients.

SUICIDE OF HOSPITALIZED PATIENT

Mental health professionals owe a duty of care to hospitalized patients to take reasonable steps to prevent suicide. In *Kockelman v. Segal*, 61 Cal. App. 4th 491, 500, 71 Cal. Rptr. 2d 552 (1998), the California Court of Appeal wrote, "[A] hospital owes its patients a duty of protection and must exercise such reasonable care as the patient's known condition might require."

SUICIDE OF RECENTLY DISCHARGED PATIENT

When a recently discharged patient commits suicide, dies in some other way, or kills someone, next of kin sometimes argue the discharge decision was negligent. (*Ex parte Kozlovski v. Altapointe Health Systems*, 2015 WL 1877656 (Ala. 2015) (doctor who participated in discharge decision had immunity from suit); *Jacoves v. United Merchandising Corp.,* 9 Cal. App. 4th 88, 11 Cal. Rptr. 2d 468 (1992); *Squeo v. Norwalk Hospital Association*, 316 Conn. 558, 113 A.3d 932 (2015)).

SUICIDE BY OUTPATIENT

It is easy to make the case that professionals must take reasonable steps to protect hospitalized patients from self-harm. Hospital staff has considerable control over inpatients. However, should the duty to protect extend to outpatients, over whom professionals have very little, if any, control? In *Kockelman v. Segal*, 61 Cal. App. 4th 491, 501, 71 Cal. Rptr. 2d 552 (1998), the California Court of Appeal said yes. The court wrote, "California courts have recognized that psychiatrists owe a duty of care, consistent with standards in the professional community, to provide appropriate treatment for potentially suicidal patients, whether the patient is hospitalized or not. There is no reasonable basis [to distinguish between inpatients and outpatients]. Indeed, it would seem almost self-evident that doctors must use reasonable care with *all* of their patients in diagnosing suicidal intent and implementing treatment plans." (*See also, Estates of Morgan v. Fairfield Family Counseling Center,* 77 Ohio St. 3d 284, 673 N.E.2d 1311 (1977)).

In *Haar v. Ulwelling*, 141 N.M. 252, 154 P.3d 67 (2007), Eric Haar committed suicide. Haar received treatment from a psychologist. As well, Haar had five office visits with Dr. Ulwelling, a psychiatrist. Dr.

Ulwelling prescribed medications. Haar expressed dissatisfaction with Dr. Ulwelling, and Haar's mother suggested he get a new doctor. Haar missed two office visits with Dr. Ulwelling. Haar was hospitalized, and treated by a different psychiatrist. Haar killed himself a month later. Haar's parents sued Dr. Ulwelling, claiming he had a duty to prevent their son's suicide. The trial judge ruled Dr. Ulwelling had no duty to prevent Haar's suicide, and the Court of Appeals affirmed, writing:

Under the circumstances, we see no affirmative duty, much less a right, on the part of Defendant to have intervened in the ongoing treatment by the other mental health care providers, treatment that Haar chose and continued with to the exclusion of Defendant and without having sought Defendant's assistance in any regard. Haar showed no interest in maintaining any semblance of a physician-patient relationship with Defendant. We therefore think it is unreasonable to place upon Defendant a requirement that he have imposed his views or treatment recommendations on Haar [or his new doctors] for the purpose of guarding against Haar's suicide. Further, under circumstances such as those in the present case, we are concerned about the consequences of burdening therapists generally with such a requirement. . . .

The once-existing special relationship and ability to control Haar's treatment disintegrated as a result of Haar's failure . . . to seek

Defendant's assistance in any regard and Haar's having chosen other mental health providers to handle his treatment and medication. (154 P.3d at 73).

F.   DUTY TO PROTECT THIRD PERSONS FROM DANGEROUS PATIENT

Generally, the law does not impose a duty on people to protect other people from the dangerous/criminal acts of third persons. (*Kim v. Budget Rent A Car System, Inc.*, 143 Wash. 2d 190, 15 P.3d 1283 (2001)). The law *does* impose a duty to protect when "a special relation exists between the actor and the third person, which imposes a duty upon the actor to control the third person's conduct." *Restatement of Torts, Second* § 315(a). A "special relation" exists between mental health professionals and clients. As a result, in some cases, mental health professionals must take steps to protect third persons from dangerous clients.

The leading authority is the California Supreme Court's decision in *Tarasoff v. Regents of the University of California*, 17 Cal. 3d 425, 551 P.2d 334, 131 Cal. Rptr. 14 (1976). The court ruled that psychotherapists have a duty to warn potential victims of dangerous clients. The court wrote, "[O]nce a therapist does in fact determine, or under applicable professional standards reasonably should have determined, that a patient poses a serious danger of violence to others, he bears a duty to exercise reasonable care to protect the foreseeable victim of that danger. While the discharge of this duty of due care will necessarily vary with the facts of each case, in each instance the adequacy of the therapist's conduct must be measured against the traditional negligence standard of the rendition of reasonable care under the circumstances." (17 Cal. 3d at 442). Failure to warn is malpractice. (*See, Ewing v. Goldstein*, 120 Cal. App. 4th 807, 15 Cal. Rptr. 3d 864 (2004)).

A duty to warn arises only when a patient threatens a third person. In *Dunnigan v. Silva*, 916 So. 2d 1166 (La. Ct. App. 2005), James Prather was civilly committed to a psychiatric hospital. Upon his release, he killed his wife and daughter, and then took his own life. In a wrongful death suit, survivors sued a doctor and the hospital for failing to inform the victims that James was released. The defendants prevailed on summary judgment because there was no evidence James made threats against his wife and daughter.

Professional organizations have recognized the duty to warn. An ethics opinion from the American Medical Association states, "When a patient threatens to inflict serious physical harm to another person or to him or herself and there is a reasonable probability that the patient may carry out the threat, the physician should take reasonable precautions for the protection of the intended victim, which may include notification of law enforcement authorities." (American Medical Association, Opinion 5.05— Confidentiality (1983, 2007)).

The *Tarasoff* duty to warn overrides confidentiality and privilege. The *Tarasoff* court wrote, "The public policy favoring protection of the confidential character of patient-psychotherapist communications must yield to the extent to which disclosure is essential to avert danger to others. The protective privilege ends where the public peril begins." (17 Cal. 3d at p. 442). In a similar vein, the Colorado Supreme Court remarked in *People v. Kailey*, 333 P.3d 89, 91 (Colo. 2014), "We hold that if a mental health treatment provider believes, using his or her professional judgment, that statements made by a patient during a therapy session threaten imminent physical violence against a specific person or persons—and accordingly trigger the provider's 'duty to warn'—the patient's threatening statements are not protected by the psychologist-patient privilege."

The *Code of Ethics* of the National Association of Social Workers grapples with *Tarasoff* as follows: "The general expectation that social workers will keep information confidential does not apply when disclosure is necessary to prevent serious, foreseeable, and imminent harm to a client or other identifiable person." (Ethical Standard 1.07(c)).

A professional who warns potential victims of a dangerous client, cannot be sued for disclosure of confidential information. (*Expose v. Thad Wilderson & Associates,* 863 N.W.2d 95 (Minn. Ct. App. 2015)).

The *Tarasoff* duty to warn is controversial. Critics argue that requiring a therapist to breach confidentiality may harm or destroy the therapist's ability to help the patient deal constructively with feelings of anger or violence. Indeed, Griffin Edwards conducted empirical research, and concluded that requiring therapists to warn potential victims may increase the murder rate! (Griffin Edwards, Doing Their Duty: An Empirical Analysis of the Unintended Effect of *Tarasoff v. Regents* on Homicidal Activity, 57 *Journal of Law and Economics* 321–345 (2014)).

About half the states have statutes on the *Tarsoff* duty to warn. (Paul B. Herbert & Kathryn A. Young, *Tarasoff* at Twenty-Five, 30 *Journal of the American Academy of Psychiatry and Law* 275–281 (2002)). The California Legislature codified *Tarasoff* in Civil Code § 43.93, which provides: "There shall be no monetary liability on the part of . . . a psychotherapist. . . . in failing to protect from a patient's threatened violent behavior or failing to predict and protect from a patient's violent behavior except if the patient has communicated to the psychotherapist a serious threat of physical violence against a reasonably identifiable victim or victims."

Arizona's law states, "There shall be no cause of action against a mental health provider nor shall legal liability be imposed for breaching a duty to prevent harm to a person caused by a patient, unless both of the following occur: (1) The patient has communicated to the mental health provider an explicit threat of imminent serious physical harm or death to a clearly identified or identifiable victim or victims, and the patient has the apparent intent and ability to carry out such threat. (2) The mental health provider fails to take reasonable precautions." (Arizona Revised Statutes § 36–517.02).

A professional with a duty to warn takes reasonable precautions by communicating the threat to identifiable victims, contacting law enforcement, initiating involuntary civil commitment proceedings, or taking other reasonable steps.

Assuming a *Tarasoff*-like duty to warn applies, and a mental health professional warns a victim or calls police, may the professional testify in later legal proceedings? The Colorado Supreme Court addressed this question in *People v. Kailey,* 333 P.3d 89 (Colo. 2014):

> While virtually all jurisdictions have acknowledged some form of the duty to warn, various jurisdictions have nevertheless strenuously disagreed whether mental health treatment providers can testify about threatening statements made by their patients when these statements have been disclosed pursuant to the duty to warn. For example, in *United States v. Hayes*, 227 F.3d 578, 586 (6th Cir. 2000), the Sixth Circuit Court of Appeals held that even if a mental health treatment provider warns potential victims and law enforcement about a patient's threatening statements, the provider is still barred from testifying about these statements in court. In contrast, in *United States v. Auster*, 517 F.3d 312, 317 (5th Cir. 2008), the Fifth Circuit Court of Appeals held that the testimonial privilege does not bar mental health treatment providers from testifying about threatening statements

that the providers disclosed pursuant to their duty to warn.

We conclude that the Fifth Circuit's approach best harmonizes the legislature's sometimes-competing objectives in establishing the psychologist-patient privilege and the duty to warn. Specifically, we hold that threatening statements disclosed pursuant to that duty are not subject to the privilege because (1) such statements are not confidential as a matter of law, and (2) barring them would be inconsistent with legislative intent. (333 P.3d at 94).

The *Restatement of Torts, Third* has useful examples where a duty to warn may arise:

Dr. Jones, a psychiatrist, sees a patient, Todd. During the course of therapy, Todd expresses a desire to harm his former girlfriend, Caroline, who had severed their relationship. Dr. Jones concludes that Todd poses a real risk of acting on his threat. Although Todd does not name his girlfriend in his sessions with Dr. Jones, her name was in Todd's medical records based on an initial history completed when Todd first became a patient of Dr. Jones. Dr. Jones does nothing to notify Caroline or otherwise take steps to protect her. Todd physically harms Caroline, who sues Dr. Jones. Dr. Jones owes Caroline a duty of reasonable care and is subject to liability for Caroline's harm.

Steve, a 14-year-old having adolescent adjustment difficulties, is referred to Dr. Cress, a psychologist. Dr. Cress treats Steve for several months, concluding that Steve suffers from mild depression and deficits in peer social skills. Steve occasionally expresses generalized anger at his circumstances in life but never blames others or gives any other indication that he might act violently, and Dr. Cress has no reason to think that Steve poses a risk of harm to others. Steve hacks his parents to death with a scythe. Dr. Cress had no duty to Steve's parents and is not subject to liability to the administrators of their estates.

Dr. Strand, a clinical psychologist, becomes aware, during the course of counseling, that a patient, Lester, is sexually abusing his eight-year-old stepdaughter, Kelly. Dr. Strand does not communicate this information to Kelly's mother or to appropriate officials of the state Department of Social Services, or take any other steps to prevent Lester from continuing his sexual assaults on Kelly. Dr. Strand owes a duty of reasonable care to Kelly and is subject to liability for the harm due to Lester's continuing abuse of her.

Perrin suffers from schizophrenia, which can generally be controlled with medication. However, Perrin intermittently, with no apparent pattern, stops taking his medication. On these occasions he suffers severe delusions and frequently believes that he is under attack by various inanimate objects. Several of these episodes are punctuated by aggressive and threatening behavior that leads Dr. Hillsley, his treating psychotherapist, to believe that Perrin cannot live on his own and poses a significant danger to others unless he continues taking his medication. Dr. Hillsley receives a call from Perrin one Saturday morning, during which it becomes clear that he is not taking his medicine. Perrin requests an immediate office visit and tells Dr. Hillsley that pedestrians on the street are carrying surgical instruments with which to investigate Perrin's brain; Perrin assures Dr. Hillsley that he will retaliate in kind at the first provocation. Dr. Hillsley, not wanting to be bothered on the weekend, declines to meet with Perrin to evaluate whether he should be involuntarily committed or to recommend that Perrin seek an evaluation at the local psychiatric hospital. Instead, he suggests that Perrin go home and call his office on a weekday to make an appointment to see him during regular hours. Instead of going home, Perrin grabs Jake, a passerby on the street, and stabs him in the neck. Dr. Hillsley has a special relationship with Perrin and a duty of reasonable care to Jake and others put at risk by Perrin. Dr. Hillsley is subject to liability for Jake's harm. (§ 41, pp. 69–71).

John Monahan draws on his experience consulting on *Tarasoff* cases to offer the following advice:

Most of the *Tarasoff*-like cases on which I have worked have faulted clinicians not for making an inaccurate prediction but for failing to gather information that would have made a reasonable effort at prediction possible. There are generally four sources in which relevant information can be found: in the records of past treatment, in the records of current treatment, from interviewing the patient, and from interviewing significant others. In some criminal contexts (*e.g.*, assessments for suitability for release on parole or from insanity commitment) additional records in the form of police and probation reports, arrest records, and trial transcripts may also be available and should be consulted. But in the civil context, these records are generally not available to clinicians.

John Monahan, Limiting Therapist Exposure to *Tarasoff* Liability: Guidelines for Risk Containment. In Donald N. Bershoff (Ed.), *Ethical Conflicts in Psychology* (APA 4th ed. 2008) (first published in 48 *American Psychologist* 242–250).

In *Thapar v. Zezulka*, 994 S.W.3d 635 (Tex. 1999), the Texas Supreme Court rejected the duty to warn, writing, "We refrain from imposing on mental-health professionals a duty to warn third parties of a patient's threats." (p. 636).

G. ABANDONMENT VS. TERMINATION OF TREATMENT

Bringing therapy to an end is part of therapy, not an afterthought. Thomas Nagy writes, "Psychologists generally terminate treatment when the client or patient (a) no longer needs the services, (b) is not likely to benefit, or (c) is being harmed by continuing. A fourth situation not mentioned in the Ethics Code would be a judgment call by the therapist that the client or patient is no longer benefiting from the services." (Thomas F. Nagy, *Essential Ethics for Psychologists: A Primer for Understanding and Mastering Core Issues,* p. 194 (American Psychological Association 2011)).

Samuel Knapp and Leon VandeCreek write, "Except when institutional policies state otherwise, psychologists may refuse to treat potential patients for any reason, including their perceived ability to pay for services. Once treatment has started, however, they do not have an unqualified right to terminate unless the treatment is completed; the patient ends the relationship; or the psychologist recommends alternative services and provides termination counseling, unless precluded by the actions of the clients or third-party payers." (Samuel J. Knapp & Leon D. VandeCreek, *Practical Ethics for Psychologists: A Positive Approach,* p. 196 (American Psychological Association 2006)).

Competent termination of treatment looks nothing like abandonment. Samuel Knapp and Leon VandeCreek advise, "Abandonment means termination of a patient when the psychologist knows or should have known that more treatment was needed." (Samuel J. Knapp & Leon D. VandeCreek, *Practical Ethics for Psychologists: A Positive Approach,* p. 197 (American Psychological Association 2006)). The New Jersey Supreme Court defined abandonment in *Marshall v. Klebanov,* 188

N.J. 23, 902 A.2d 873, 879 (2006), "A mental health practitioner abandons a patient by failing to continue to provide service to the patient when it is still needed in a case for which the physician has assumed responsibility and from which the physician has not been properly relieved." It is malpractice to abandon a client when the abandonment harms the client.

H. DUTY TO REPORT CHILD ABUSE AND NEGLECT

Every state requires professionals who interact with children to report suspected child abuse and neglect. The reporting duty applies to social workers, physicians, dentists, nurses, psychologists, counselors, teachers, law enforcement officers, and child care professionals.

The duty to report suspected maltreatment is triggered when a professional possesses the level of suspicion specified in the reporting law. Reporting laws differ slightly in the words used to describe the triggering level of suspicion. Common phrases include "cause to believe," "reasonable cause to believe," "known or suspected abuse," and "observation or examination that discloses evidence of abuse." (*See Thomas v. Sumner,* 341 P.3d 390 (Wyo. 2015)).

Although words differ, the basic thrust of reporting laws is the same across the United States: A report is required when a professional has information that would lead a competent professional to believe maltreatment is likely. Whether the triggering level of suspicion exists depends on the facts of the case, interpreted through the lens of experience and judgment.

Although it is sometimes difficult to determine when the triggering level of suspicion exists, one thing is clear: The reporting law does not require the professional to be certain maltreatment occurred. Reporting is triggered by suspicion, not certainty. A professional who postpones reporting until all doubt is eliminated violates the reporting law. Moreover, a mandated reporter is required to report suspected maltreatment whether or not the professional believes reporting is wise. When maltreatment is suspected, reporting is mandatory, not discretionary.

The reporting law leaves final decisions about whether maltreatment occurred to investigating authorities, not reporters. Mandated reporters should report their suspicions, and leave investigation to child protective services or police. This does not mean professionals ask no questions. Alternatives to maltreatment are considered. The point is that in-depth investigation and decision making about maltreatment is reserved for child protective services and law enforcement—not mandated reporters. Once the triggering level of suspicion is reached, the reporter turns the matter over to the authorities.

Intentional failure to report suspected child abuse or neglect is a crime. In addition to criminal liability, if a mandated reporter does not report suspected maltreatment—and the child is further abused or killed—the professional can be sued for malpractice. (*Landeros v. Flood,* 17 Cal. 3d 399, 551 P.2d 389, 131

Cal. Rptr. 69 (1976)). Several states have laws specifically authorizing lawsuits against professionals who willfully fail to report.

In a small number of cases, angry parents sued professionals who reported suspected maltreatment. Such lawsuits are generally dismissed because the child abuse reporting law gives professionals immunity from civil liability. (*See, e.g., Marks v. Tenbrunsel*, 910 So. 2d 1255 (Ala. 2005); *Dwight R. v. Christy B.*, 212 Cal. App. 4th 697, 151 Cal. Rptr. 3d 406 (2013); J.S. v. Berla, 456 S.W.3d 19 (Ky Ct. App. 2015)).

I.   CIVIL RIGHTS VIOLATIONS

Occasionally, individuals sue mental health professionals for alleged violations of civil rights. When a jail or prison inmate commits suicide, for example, surviving family members may utilize 42 U.S.C. § 1983 to assert that mental health professionals working for the facility failed to provide proper treatment or supervision. (*See Perez v. Oakland County*, 466 F.3d 416 (6th Cir. 2006)). Typically, in such cases, mental health defendants have qualified immunity. (*Miller v. Harbaugh*, 698 F.3d 956 (7th Cir. 2012); *Comstock v. McCrary,* 273 F.3d 693 (6th Cir. 2002)).

J.   COURT-APPOINTED EXPERTS HAVE IMMUNITY

Professionals appointed by a judge to evaluate an individual, prepare a report, and/or testify, generally have immunity from suit for court-related activities.

(*J.S. v. Berla*, 456 S.W.3d 19 (Ky. Ct. App. 2015)). As the Seventh Circuit put it in *Cooney v. Rossiter*, 583 F.3d 967 (7th Cir. 2009), "Court-appointed experts, including psychiatrists, are absolutely immune from liability for damages when they act at the court's direction. They are arms of the court, much like special masters, and deserve protection from harassment by disappointed litigants, just as judges do." (p. 970). Similarly, the Louisiana Court of Appeal stated in *Faust v. Pesses*, 164 So. 3d 920 (La. Ct. App. 2015), "Louisiana law is clear and unambiguous that a court-appointed expert enjoys absolute immunity from suit for services provided pursuant to that appointment." (*See also, Diehl v. Danuloff*, 242 Mich. App. 120, 618 N.W.2d 83 (2000)).

Child custody cases in family court can breed incalculable anger and heartache. When a mental health professional is appointed by the family court judge to conduct a custody evaluation, the professional typically enjoys absolute immunity from civil liability. A mental health professional who is not court-appointed lacks absolute immunity. It is not surprising that many mental health professionals will only accept custody cases when they are appointed by the court.

K. DUAL RELATIONSHIPS AND BOUNDARY CROSSINGS

In the literature on ethics in psychotherapy, no issue garners more attention than dual relationships, or, as they are also called, multiple relationships. Ofer Zur defines dual relationship as "any situation in which multiple roles exist between a therapist and a client." (Ofer Zur, *Boundaries in Psychotherapy: Ethical and Clinical Explorations*, p. 21 (American Psychological Association 2007)). The American Psychological Association (APA) *Code of Ethics* states, "A multiple relationship occurs when a psychologist is in a professional role with a person and (1) at the same time is in another role with the same person, (2) at the same time is in a relationship with a person closely associated with or related to the person with whom the psychologist has the professional relationship, or (3) promises to enter into another relationship in the future with the person or a person closely associated with or related to the person." (Ethical Standard 3.05(a)). Examples of dual relationships include providing psychotherapy to a friend or family member, sexual relationship with a client, engaging in business with a client, and switching from a therapeutic to a forensic role.

With dual relationships, a mental health professional occupies two roles at once. With boundary crossings, by contrast, a professional occupies only one role, the clinical role, but engages conduct that may cross personal, professional, ethical, or, in rare cases, legal boundaries. Zur clarifies the distinction between dual relations and boundary crossings:

> It is important to differentiate between boundary crossings such as therapeutic touch, clinically driven self-disclosure, home visits, and gift exchanges, which do not entail a secondary

relationship and those associations that involve dual relationships. Therapists in the former situations operate exclusively in their clinical capacity and, therefore, these situations are not considered dual relationships. For the same reasons, attending a client's wedding or self-disclosing for clinical reasons rather than social ones does not constitute social or other dual relationships. However, if self-disclosure or attending the client's wedding takes place in the course of a social relationship or as part of a community relationship between the therapist and client, it constitutes a dual relationship. Incidental, chance encounters between therapists and clients outside the therapy room that are not part of a social, collegial, or business connection do not constitute dual relationships. (pp. 21–22).

Not all dual relations violate ethical standards. (APA *Code of Ethics*, Ethical Standard 3.05(a)). Thomas Nagy writes, "Not every multiple-role relationship is unethical, but when a psychologist's objectivity and competence are compromised, the psychologist may find that personal needs and ambitions surface, diminishing the quality of his or her work." (Thomas F. Nagy, *Essential Ethics for Psychologists: A Primer for Understanding and Mastering Core Issues,* p. 37 (American Psychological Association 2011)).

Mental health professionals think twice before entering dual relationships. As the APA *Code of Ethics* puts it, "A psychologist refrains from entering into a multiple relationship if the multiple relationship could reasonably be expected to impair the psychologist's objectivity, competence, or effectiveness in performing his or her functions as a psychologist, or otherwise risks exploitation or harm to the person with whom the professional relationship exists. Multiple relationships that would not reasonably be expected to cause impairment or risk exploitation or harm are not unethical." (Ethical Standard 3.05(a)).

Turning from dual relations to boundary crossings, mental health professionals consider carefully whether to cross boundaries. Samuel Knapp and Leon VandeCreek state, "Some boundary crossings, such as sex with a patient, are always boundary violations. Other boundary crossings, such as therapist self-disclosure, may be violations, benign, or even helpful to the patient, depending on the circumstances. Psychologists need not develop rigid stances, but they should use their clinical judgment to determine when such boundary crossings may be therapeutically indicated." (Samuel J. Knapp & Leon D. VandeCreek, *Practical Ethics for Psychologists: A Positive Approach,* p. 76 (American Psychological Association 2006)).

It is unethical to have sex with a current client. (*See* American Association for Marriage and Family Therapy, *Code of Ethics* Principle 1.4 (2012)). The *Code of Ethics* of the National Association of Social workers states, "Social workers should under no circumstances engage in sexual activities or sexual contact with current clients, whether such contact is consensual or forced" (Ethical Standard 1.09(a)). In *Dresser v. Board of Medical Quality Assurance*, 130 Cal. App. 3d 506, 181 Cal. Rptr. 797 (1982), a therapist's license was revoked for having sex with two clients the therapist was seeing for, of all things, psychosexual problems!

What about sex with former clients? Not a good idea. The American Association for Marriage and Family Therapy states that a minimum of two years should elapse after therapy ends. (American Association for Marriage and Family Therapy, *Code of Ethics,* Principle 1.5 (2012)). In *Leon v. Ohio Board of Psychology,* 590 N.E.2d 1223, 1226 (Ohio 1992), the Ohio Supreme Court ruled that waiting seven months after treatment ended to begin a sexual relationship was not sufficient time to avoid discipline. The court wrote, "It takes no citation of authority to safely state that sexual relations between any professional and a client or immediate ex-client are universally prohibited by the ethical regulations of practically every profession."

Having sex with a client is virtually always malpractice. In *Dupree v. Giugliano*, 87 A.D.3d 975, 929 N.Y.S.2d 305 (2011), the Appellate Division of the New York Supreme Court quoted an expert witness on the special relationship between clients and mental health professionals, "The plaintiff's expert testified that because of the particularly sensitive nature of the relationship between a mental health provider and a patient, including the emotional dependence of the patient on the provider, a sexual relationship between the patient and the provider is very likely to harm the patient. Consequently, a sexual relationship between a mental health provider and a patient is a departure from the standard of care. . . . [A] sexual relationship between [a mental health] provider and a patient violates the trust that lies at the heart of the relationship." (929 N.Y.S.2d at 307–308). The New York appellate court approved punitive damages for a prolonged sexual relationship that "evinced a gross indifference to his client's wellbeing." (Id. at 308).

In *L.L. v. Medical Protective Company,* 362 N.W.2d 174 (Wis. Ct. App. 1984), a woman hired a psychiatrist to help her with "difficulty maintaining healthy interpersonal relationships, particularly with men." (p. 457). During therapy, the psychiatrist had the patient orally copulate him. The patient sued for malpractice.

In *Disciplinary Counsel v. Bunstine,* 995 N.E.2d 184 (Ohio 2013), a lawyer was suspended for a year after soliciting sex from a client in a child custody case. The lawyer offered to "make other arrangements" for payment of the fee, instructing the client to answer her door naked.

In some states, it is a crime for a mental health professional to have sex with a client. (*State v. Edouard,* 854 N.W.2d 421 (Iowa 2014)).

The Pennsylvania Supreme Court addressed an important aspect of sexual relations with clients in *Thierfelder v. Wolfert,* 617 Pa. 295, 52 A.3d 1251 (2012). In a thorough opinion canvasing the law across the country, the court observed that it is not necessarily malpractice for a medical doctor who is *not* a mental health provider to have sex with a patient. The rule against sex with clients applies to mental health professionals because of the special relationship these professionals have with clients.

What should the outcome be when a "regular" medical doctor "provides incidental mental health treatment to a patient"? (52 A.3d at 1253). The Pennsylvania Supreme Court ruled that, on the facts in *Wolfert,* a doctor would not be held to the standard required of mental health professionals.

L.   CLIENT CRIMINAL CONDUCT

A client was in therapy with a clinical social worker for ten years, from ages seven to seventeen. During treatment, the client revealed that he occasionally viewed child pornography on his computer. According to the client, the social worker failed to address the client's interest in child pornography, and, because of that failure, the client continued viewing pornography. Two years after therapy ended, police raided the former client's home and seized child pornography. The former client was charged with possession of child pornography. The former client sued the social worker, claiming that the social worker's failure to treat his interest in child pornography led to his continued viewing and eventual arrest and prosecution. In other words, the former client blamed the therapist for the client's *own criminal conduct!* These are the facts of the Connecticut Supreme Court's decision in *Greenwald v. Van Handel*, 311 Conn. 370, 88 A.3d 467 (2014), where the court stated the issue to be "whether it would violate public policy of this state to allow the plaintiff, Lee Greenwald, to maintain a professional negligence action against the defendant, David Van Handel, a licensed clinical social worker, on the basis of allegations that the defendant negligently failed to treat the plaintiff after he disclosed to the defendant that he has viewed child pornography." (88 A.3d at 469). The Supreme Court ruled "it clearly would violate public policy to impose a duty on the defendant in the present case to protect the plaintiff from injuries arising from his potential criminal prosecution for the illegal downloading, viewing and/or possession of child pornography." (Id.). The Connecticut court joined other courts in the position "that a plaintiff cannot maintain a tort action for injuries that are sustained as the direct result of his or her knowing and intentional participation in a criminal act." (Id. at 377).

In *Burcina v. Ketchikan*, 902 P.2d 817 (Alaska 1995), a patient with a long psychiatric and substance abuse history set fire to a mental health center. He was convicted of arson. Later, apparently failing to appreciate the irony, he sued the center he burned, and his psychiatrist, claiming he received negligent treatment "which aggravated his mental illness and caused him to set the fire." (902 P.2d at 818). Unimpressed, the Alaska Supreme Court wrote, "This court has recognized the public policy principle which precludes a person who has been convicted of a crime from imposing liability on others for the consequences of that antisocial conduct. (Id. at 820).

In *Rimert v. Mortell*, 680 N.E.2d 867 (Ind. Ct. App. 1997) Gary Rimert was psychiatrically hospitalized. After a time, Rimert was discharged to the care of his parents. Rimert borrowed the family car, drove to his grandparents' home, and stabbed them to death, along with two neighbors. Rimert was charged with murder, and found guilty but mentally ill. He was sentenced to life in prison. Rimert's conservator sued the treating psychiatrist for discharging Rimert, seeking damages for "loss of enjoyment of life" due to being locked up. Rejecting the claim, the Indiana Court of Appeal followed the general rule barring "actions seeking damages which were a direct result of the injured party's knowing and intentional participation in a criminal act." (680 N.E.2d at 872).

See also, Cole v. Taylor, 301 N.W.2d 766 (Iowa 1981); *Guillie v. Comprehensive Addiction Programs, Inc.*, 735 So.2d 775 (La. Ct. App. 1999); *Glazier v. Lee*, 171 Mich. App. 216, 429 N.W.2d 857 (1988).

M. IMMUNITY

At several places in the book, reference is made to immunity from liability. This paragraph briefly summarizes immunity. Mental health professional appointed by a court to conduct evaluations, write reports for the court, and testify, generally have absolute immunity from liability for court-related activities. Statutes grant immunity for certain activities, such as reporting suspected child abuse. (*Nelson v. Lindaman*, 867 N.W.2d 1 (Iowa 2015)). Professionals employed by government who are sued for civil rights violations, often have qualified immunity. The Eighth Circuit explained in *Ransom v. Grisafe,* 790 F.3d 804 (8th Cir. 2015), "Qualified immunity protects government officials from liability for civil damages insofar as their conduct does not violate clearly established statutory or constitutional rights of which a reasonable person would have known."

CHAPTER 7

DISCRIMINATION AGAINST MENTALLY ILL AND INTELLECTUALLY DISABLED

There is a long and sorry history of discrimination against disabled persons. In the Americans with Disabilities Act, Congress found, "[H]istorically, society has tended to isolate and segregate individuals with disabilities. . . . [D]iscrimination against individuals with disabilities persists. . . ." (42 U.S.C. § 12101(a)(2) and (3)). Many federal and state laws prohibit discrimination against the disabled. This chapter introduces the most well-known laws.

A. AMERICANS WITH DISABILITIES ACT

The Americans with Disabilities Act (ADA) prohibits discrimination against disabled individuals who are covered by the Act. (42 U.S.C. § 12112(a)). The ADA forbids discrimination in employment, services offered by government, and public accommodations. (*Tennessee v. Lane*, 541 U.S. 509, 516, 124 S. Ct. 1978 (2004)). For example, the ADA applies to bar examinations. (*In re Henry*, 841 N.W.2d 471 (S.D. 2013)).

Courts have applied the ADA to "social services; access to public areas and public meetings; arrests; education; housing; loans; and transportation, to name a few." (Dale Margolin, No Chance to Prove Themselves: The Rights of Mentally Disabled Parents Under the Americans with Disabilities Act and State Law, 15 *Virginia Journal of Social Policy and Law* 112 (2007)).

The ADA defines disability as "a physical or mental impairment that substantially limits one or more major life activities. . . ." (42 U.S.C. § 12102(a)(A)). The ADA covers mental illness. (*Jacobs v. N.C. Administrative Office of the Courts,* 780 F.3d 562 (4th Cir. 2015) (social anxiety disorder); *McMillan v. City of New York,* 711 F.3d 120 (2d Cir. 2013) (schizophrenia); *Taylor v. Phoenixville School District,* 184 F.3d 296 (3d Cir. 1999) (bipolar)). The ADA's implementing regulations state that mental impairment includes, "Any mental or psychological disorder, such as an intellectual disability (formerly termed 'mental retardation'), organic brain syndrome, emotional or mental illness, and specific learning disabilities." (29 C.F.R. § 1630.2(h)(2)).

The ADA and implementing regulations define major life activities to include caring for oneself, working, concentrating, thinking, interacting with others, and communicating. (42 U.S.C. § 12102(2)(A); 29 C.F.R. § 1630.2(h)(2)(i)).

Not everyone with a disability has rights under the ADA. The Act extends to disabled persons who are "qualified." (42 U.S.C. § 12111(8)). William Goren explains:

A person may have a disability and not be protected under the ADA because he or she is not qualified. Qualified has two different meanings under the ADA depending upon whether Title I (which applies to employers of 15 or more employees) or Title II (which applies to governmental entities regardless of size) is at issue. Under Title I of the ADA, a person with a disabling condition is qualified if he or she satisfies the requisite skill, experience, and education requirements of the position and can, with or without reasonable accommodation, perform the essential functions of the job. . . .

With respect to Title II of the ADA, a person is considered to be otherwise qualified if he or she can, with or without reasonable modification of rules, policies, or practices; the removal of architectural, communication, or transportation barriers; or the provision of auxiliary aids and services, meet the essential eligibility requirements for receiving services or participating in programs or activities provided by a public entity.

William D. Green, *Understanding the ADA,* p. 9 (4th ed. 2013).

The fact that a person who is covered by the ADA is denied a job or fired does not mean the person suffered discrimination. Thus, it is not discrimination to deny or terminate employment to someone who cannot do the job, even with reasonable accommodation. (*Walz v. Ameriprise Financial*, 779 F.3d 842 (8th Cir. 2015) (person with bipolar disorder could not perform the task for which she was hired)).

Reasonable accommodations for disabled individuals include making facilities accessible, job restructuring, and similar accommodations, depending on the needs of the individual. (42 U.S.C. § 12111(9)).

In *Stern v. St. Anthony's Health Center*, 788 F.3d 276 (7th Cir. 2015), Dr. Stern was a psychologist who held the highly responsible position of Chief Psychologist for an acute-care facility offering outpatient and inpatient psychological services. Dr. Alton supervised other mental health professionals and provided clinical care for children. Sadly, Dr. Alton slowly developed dementia that made it impossible for him to perform his duties. The doctor was evaluated, and the evaluator concluded Dr. Alton was incapable of doing his job. The doctor was let go, and sued his employer under the ADA. The Seventh Circuit ruled against Dr. Alton because, even with accommodations, his condition prevented him from performing the essential functions of his position.

The ADA does not cover individuals who are disabled due to current use of illegal drugs. (42 U.S.C. § 12114(a)). On the other hand, the ADA does cover people who successfully complete drug rehabilitation, as well as those who are working to "kick the habit" by stopping drug use and participating in treatment. (42 U.S.C. § 12114(b)).

A quote at the beginning of this section states that some courts have applied the ADA when police arrest a person who is mentally ill. The applicability of the ADA to interactions between police and the mentally ill is an evolving area of law. In *De Boise v. Taser Intern., Inc.,* 760 F.3d 892, 899 (8th Cir. 2014), the Eighth Circuit stated, "We have said that inquiry into whether officers reasonably accommodated the individual is highly fact-specific and varies depending on the circumstances of each case, including the exigent circumstances presented by criminal activity and safety concerns and that we will not second guess an officer's judgments where an officer is presented with exigent or unexpected circumstances." In 2015, the U.S. Supreme Court had an opportunity to decide whether the ADA applies to arrests. In *City and County of San Francisco, California v. Sheehan*, 135 S. Ct. 1765 (2015), the Court declined the opportunity, leaving open the question whether the ADA applies to arrests.

The facts of the *Sheehan* case demonstrate why it is difficult to tell when the ADA should apply to police work. Teresa Sheehan suffered from shizoaffective disorder. She lived in a San Francisco group home for individuals with mental illness. A social worker at the home knocked on Sheehan's door to check on her. Sheehan had stopped taking her medication, stopped communicating with her psychiatrist, and was not eating or changing her clothes. When no one responded to the knock, the social worker used a key to open the door. At first, Sheehan would not answer questions. Then, she sprang up and yelled, "Get out of here! You don't have a warrant! I have a knife, and I'll kill you if I have to." The social worker retreated, and Sheehan slammed the door. The social worker realized Sheehan needed help, and that he needed help to help her. The social worker cleared the building of other people. Then he filled out the paperwork for emergency civil commitment. The worker called the police department and asked for help to take Sheehan to the hospital.

Two police officers responded to the group home. The officers and the social worker went to Sheehan's room and knocked, but got no answer. The officers used the social worker's key to open the door and enter the room. Sheehan reacted violently. She grabbed a knife with a five inch blade and approached the officers, yelling, "I'm going to kill you. I don't need help. Get out." The officers left the room, and Sheehan closed the door.

The officers called for backup. They were concerned that Sheehan might gather additional weapons or flee out a window. The officers decided they could not wait for backup, and they needed to get control of Sheehan. As the Supreme Court put it, "In making that decision, they did not pause to consider whether Sheehan's disability should be accommodated." (135 S. Ct. at 1771).

The plan was for one officer to push the door open while the other used pepper spray on Sheehan. The officers drew their pistols and entered. Sheehan had the knife in her hand, and yelled at them to get out. One officer began pepper straying Sheehan in the face, but she would not drop the knife. When Sheehan was only a few feet from the officers, they shot her multiple times.

Fortunately, Sheehan survived. She sued the city and the officers, claiming they violated the ADA by taking her into custody in a way that did not accommodate her disability. The trial court granted summary judgment, holding that police officers making an arrest are not required to comply with the ADA before taking steps to protect themselves and others. On appeal, the Ninth Circuit vacated the summary judgment, concluding it was "for a jury to decide whether San Francisco should have accommodated Sheehan by, for instance, respecting her comfort zone, engaging in non-threatening communications and using the passage of time to defuse the situation rather than precipitating a deadly confrontation." (135 S. Ct. 1765, 1772 (2015). The Supreme Court granted certiorari, but then thought better of it and decided not to decide whether the ADA applies to arrests.

America's juvenile courts have authority to protect abused and neglected children. When a juvenile court finds that a child has been abused or neglected, the parents generally are offered services to help remedy the problems that led to maltreatment. A number of courts have held that the ADA applies to services ordered by juvenile court. (*See Lucy J. v. State Department of Health and Social Services*, 244 P.3d 1099 (Alaska 2010); *In re Adoption of Gregory*, 434 Mass. 117, 747 N.E.2d 120 (2001); *In re Terry*, 240 Mich. App. 14, 610 N.W.2d 563 (2000)).

In cases where services for maltreating parents do not succeed, the government may ask the juvenile court to permanently sever the parent-child relationship—terminate parental rights. In a few termination of parental rights cases, parents argued that the ADA applied, and barred termination. Courts generally rule that the ADA does not apply in termination of parental rights litigation. (*See S.G. v. Barbour County Department of Human Resources*, 148 So. 3d 439 (Ala. 2014); *In re C.Z.*, 2015 WL

3776549 (Colo. Ct. App. 2015); *In re Joseph W. Jr.*, 146 Conn. App. 468, 78 A.3d 276 (2013)).

University students with mental health issues occasionally use the ADA to argue their school discriminated against them. (*See* Barbara A. Lee, Dealing with Students with Psychiatric Disorders on Campus: Legal Compliance and Prevention Strategies, 40 *Journal of College and University Law* 425 (2014)).

B.   SECTION 504

The Rehabilitation Act of 1973 was the first federal civil rights law to provide broad protection to disabled persons. Section 504 of the Act provides, "No other qualified handicapped individual in the United States . . . shall, solely by reason of her or his handicap, be excluded from the participation in, be denied the benefits of, or be subjected to discrimination under any program or activity receiving Federal financial assistance." (29 U.S.C. § 794(a)). A person is covered by the Act when she has a physical or mental disability that substantially limits one or more major life activities. Section 504 works in tandem with the ADA.

It is common for plaintiffs to invoke multiple federal and state antidiscrimination statutes in the same lawsuit. Thus, plaintiffs often sue under the ADA and Section 504. (*See, e.g., Cohon v. New Mexico Department of Health*, 646 F.3d 717 (10th Cir. 2011); *Andersen v. North Shore Long Island Jewish Healthcare System's Zucker Hillside Hospital*, 2015 WL 1443254 (E.D. N.Y. 2015); *Nikolich v. Village of*

Arlington Heights, 870 F. Supp. 2d 556, 562 (N.D. Ill. 2012)).

The Federal Fair Housing Act makes it unlawful "to discriminate in the sale or rental, or to otherwise make unavailable or deny, a dwelling to any buyer or renter because of a handicap." (42 U.S.C. § 3604(f)(1)). "Discrimination includes refusing to make reasonable accommodations necessary to afford a disabled person equal opportunity to use or enjoy a dwelling." (*Nikolich v. Village of Arlington Heights*, 870 F. Supp. 2d 556, 562 (N.D. Ill. 2012)).

C.   FAIR HOUSING ACT

As late as the 1970s, large numbers is disabled children were excluded from public schools. Disabled children who were in school, often were shortchanged. Congress passed the Individuals with Disabilities Education Act (IDEA) in 1975 to bring disabled children into America's schools, and to guarantee physically and mentally disabled children a free and appropriate public education (FAPE). (20 U.S.C. § 1400).

D.   IDEA

IDEA defines emotional disturbance as follows:

A condition exhibiting one or more of the following characteristics over a long period of time and to a marked degree that adversely affects a child's educational performance: (A) An inability to learn that cannot be explained by intellectual, sensory, or health factors. (B) An inability to build or maintain satisfactory interpersonal relationships with peers, and teachers. (C) Inappropriate types of behavior or feelings under normal circumstances. (D) A general pervasive mood of unhappiness or depression. (E) A tendency to develop physical symptoms or fears associated with personal or school problems.

Emotional disturbance includes schizophrenia. The term does not apply to children who are socially maladjusted, unless it is determined that they have an emotional disturbance.

34 C.F.R. § 300.8(c)(4).

Students who may qualify for services under the IDEA are evaluated by a team of education and related professionals. Disabled students are provided an individualized education program (IEP) that describes the educational and support services the child needs to benefit from education.

Parents who are dissatisfied with the services provided their child may request a hearing to seek different or additional services. Judicial review is available after administrative remedies are exhausted. (*See Fry v. Napoleon Community Schools*, 788 F.3d 622 (6th Cir. 2015)).

E.   STATE ANTIDISCRIMINATION LAWS

States have antidiscrimination laws that cover mental disability. (*See Mammone v. President and Fellows of Harvard College*, 446 Mass. 657, 847

N.E.2d 276 (2006)). Like the ADA, state statutes cover employment, housing, and government services.

CHAPTER 8

FINANCIAL AND MEDICAL BENEFITS FOR DISABLED PERSONS

Many disabled adults hold down jobs and support themselves and their families. Yet, thousands of seriously disabled people cannot work. Fortunately, programs exist to provide financial, medical, nutritional, and housing support for qualified disabled people. These programs are private and public. This chapter introduces the principle public programs for the disabled.

A.   SOCIAL SECURITY ACT

The Social Security Act was passed by Congress in 1935, at the height of the Great Depression, to provide financial relief for older Americans. During that time of economic crisis, the U.S. Supreme Court referred to the Social Security Act in these words, "The hope behind this statute is to save men and women from the rigors of the poor house as well as from the haunting fear that such a lot awaits them when the journey's end is near." (*Helvering v. Davis*, 301 U.S. 619, 641, 57 S. Ct. 904 (1937)).

The original Social Security Act provided retirement benefits for older workers who paid Social Security taxes. The Social Security retirement tax, called FICA—Federal Insurance Contributions Act— is still paid by workers in employment that is covered by the Social Security Act ("covered employment"). A worker who has paid sufficient FICA taxes is a "covered worker," and can receive Social Security retirement payments when the worker reaches retirement age. More than 41 million Americans receive Social Security retirement.

B.   SOCIAL SECURITY DISABILITY

In 1956, Congress amended the Social Security Act by adding disability benefits for covered workers who become disabled. Disability benefits are paid to disabled workers, surviving spouses of such workers, and children of such workers. The Social Security Act defines disability as the inability to engage in substantial gainful activity due to a medically determinable mental or physical impairment that can be expected to result in death or to last at least a year.

To determine whether an applicant for disability benefits is eligible, Social Security uses a five step sequential evaluation process. (*See Andrews v. Colvin*, 791 F.3d 923 (8th Cir. 2015)). First, is the applicant engaged is substantial gainful activity—work? If the answer is yes, then the applicant is not eligible, regardless of disability.

Second, if the applicant is not engaged in substantial gainful activity, does the applicant have a severe impairment that significantly limits the person's ability to perform work? If not, the applicant is not eligible. Substantial work activity is work that involves significant physical or mental activities. Work is "gainful" when it is for pay.

Third, if the applicant has a severe impairment, does the impairment meet or equal a disability in

Social Security's Listing of Impairments? If yes, the applicant is eligible.

The Listing of Impairment includes the following mental disorders: organic mental disorders, schizophrenia and other psychotic disorders; affective disorders (*e.g.,* bipolar) intellectual disability; anxiety-related disorders, somatoform disorders; personality disorders, and substance abuse disorders. (Alcoholism and drug addiction do not qualify).

To get a feel for the Listing of Impairments, consider the Listing for "Schizophrenic, Paranoid and Other Psychotic Disorders," which follows:

Characterized by the onset of psychotic features with deterioration from a previous level of functioning. The required level of severity for these disorders is met when the requirements of both A and B are satisfied, or when the requirements of C are satisfied:

A. Medically documented persistence, either continuous or intermittent, of one of the following:

(1) Delusions or hallucinations; or

(2) Catatonic or other grossly disorganized behavior; or

(3) Incoherence, loosening of associations, illogical thinking, or poverty of content of speech if associated with one of the following: (a) Blunt affect; or (b) Flat affect; or (c) Inappropriate affect; or

(4) Emotional withdrawal and/or isolation;

AND

B.   Resulting in at least two of the following:

(1) Marked restriction of activities of daily living; or

(2) Marked difficulties in maintaining social functioning; or

(3) Marked difficulties in maintaining concentration, persistence, or pace; or

(4) Repeated episodes of decompensation, each of extended duration;

OR

C.   Medically documented history of chronic schizophrenic, paranoid, or other psychotic disorder of at least 2 years' duration that has caused more than a minimal limitation of ability to do basic work activities, with symptoms or signs currently attenuated by medication or psychosocial support, and one of the following:

(1) Repeated episodes of decompensation, each of extended duration; or

(2) A residual disease process that has resulted in such marginal adjustment that even a minimal increase in mental demands or change in the environment would be predicted to cause the individual to decompensate; or

(3) Current history of 1 or more years' inability to function outside a highly supportive

living arrangement, with an indication of continued need for such an arrangement.

Fourth, if a severely impaired person's disability does not meet or equal a condition in the Listing of Impairments, is the disabled person able to do the kind of work she or he did previously? If the answer is yes, the applicant is not eligible.

Fifth, if the person is not able to do the kind of work done previously, does the person have the residual functional capacity, age, education, and prior experience to perform other substantial gainful activity? If the answer is yes, the person is not eligible. If the answer is no, the person is eligible.

Persons seeking disability benefits have the burden of proving eligibility. The applicant must provide medical evidence consisting of signs and symptoms, laboratory findings (including psychological testing), other medical evidence, and the testimony of witnesses, including the applicant. If the person makes it to step four of the sequential evaluation process, and proves that she or he is unable to perform work done in the past, then the burden of proof shifts to Social Security to prove that the person can do other work.

The entity that makes initial recommendations on applications for Social Security disability is a state agency called the Disability Determination Section (DDS). Based on DDS's recommendation, Social Security approves or denies applications.

When an application is rejected, the first step in the appeal process is to request reconsideration. If reconsideration is unsuccessful (usually the case), the next step is a hearing before an Administrative Law Judge (ALJ) from the Office of Disability Adjudication and Review. Denial by an ALJ can be followed by appeal to the Social Security Appeals Council. Finally, a dissatisfied applicant can file in Federal Court. The Federal Court's role is limited to determining whether the decision on disability is supported by substantial evidence. If so, the court defers to the decision.

C.   SUPPLEMENTAL SECURITY INCOME DISABILITY

The Supplemental Security Income (SSI) program became law in 1974, and provides disability benefits to poor children and adults. As well, SSI pays financial benefits to low income adults over 65 who are not disabled.

The same disability definitions and standards are used for Social Security Disability and SSI Disability.

D.   STATE AND PRIVATE DISABILITY

States and the federal government provide disability benefits and disability retirement for government workers. As well, individuals can purchase private disability insurance. Government disability programs generally cover mental as well as physical illness and injury. (*See, e.g., Patterson v. Board of Trustees, State Police Retirement System*, 194 N.J. 29, 942 A.2d 782 (2008)).

E. MEDICAL BENEFITS FOR THE DISABLED

In addition to Social Security retirement and disability, and SSI Disability, the Social Security Act provides medical benefits, including Medicare for individuals over age 65. Disabled individuals under 65 also get Medicare.

Medicaid provides medical coverage for the poor.

F. PARITY IN HEALTH INSURANCE

It was once common for insurance companies to exclude or severely limit mental health coverage, as compared to coverage for physical ailments and surgery. To reduce this disparity, Congress passed the Mental Health Parity and Addiction Equity Act of 2008. Although the Act is complicated, and does not apply to all Americans, it strives for parity regarding copayments, deductibles, number of doctor visits allowed, and lifetime dollar limits on care.

G. WORKERS' COMPENSATION

Worker's compensation laws generally cover job-related psychological injuries. (*See Gartrell v. Department of Correction*, 259 Conn. 29, 787 A.2d 541 (2002). In *Bailey v. Republic Engineered Steels, Inc.*, 91 Ohio St. 3d 38, 741 N.E.2d 121 (2001), Bailey was at work when he accidentally ran over and killed a co-worker. As a result, Bailey fell into a severe depression, and sought workers' compensation from his employer. The Ohio Supreme Court ruled, "We conclude that the legislature's intent was to allow compensation in cases where an employee suffers a mental injury caused by a coworker's physical injury. This construction of the statute fulfills the compensatory objective and humanitarian nature of the Act. In fact, to deny coverage to a claimant who has suffered a psychiatric injury as a result of a physical injury to a coworker would frustrate the very purpose of the Act, which is to compensate workers who are injured as a result of the requirements of their employment." (741 N.E.2d at 124).

INDEX

References are to Pages

COMPETENCE

COMPETENCE TO STAND TRIAL,

CONFIDENTIALITY (Chapter 2)

MARRIAGE AND FAMILY THERAPIST, 2

MEDICAID, 231

MEDICARE, 231

MEDICATIONS, 19, 33–34, 126–127, 151, 184

MENTAL ILLNESS, 8–33

MENTAL RETARDATION (See Intellectual Disability)

MENTAL STATUS EXAM, 15–16, 30

MINI-MENTAL STATUS EXAM, 30–31

MISTAKE OF FACT (See Criminal Law)

MODEL PENAL CODE (See Criminal Law and Insanity)

MUNCHAUSEN SYNDROME BY PROXY, 23, 70

NEGLIGENT INFLICTION OF EMOTIONAL DISTRESS, 179–180

NEURODEVELOPMENTAL DISORDERS, 16–17

NONORGANIC FAILURE TO THRIVE, 23

NURSE, 2

OBSESSIVE-COMPULSIVE DISORDER, 21–22

OUTPATIENT COMMITMENT (See Civil Commitment)

PARAPHILIA, 24

PARENS PATRIA AUTHORITY (See Civil Commitment)

PARITY IN INSURANCE, 231

PATIENT-LITIGANT EXCEPTION (See Privilege)

PHYSICIAN-PATIENT PRIVILEGE (See Privilege)